THE GREAT LIVES SERIES

Great Lives biographies shed an exciting new light on the many dynamic men and women whose actions, visions, and dedication to an ideal have influenced the course of history. Their ambitions, dreams, successes, and failures, the controversies they faced and the obstacles they overcame are the true stories behind these distinguished world leaders, explorers, and great Americans.

Other biographies in the Great Lives Series

ACKNOWLEDGMENT

A special thanks to educators Dr. Frank Moretti, Ph.D., Associate Headmaster of the Dalton School in New York City; Dr. Paul Mattingly, Ph.D., Professor of History at New York University; and Barbara Smith, M.S., Assistant Superintendent of the Los Angeles Unified School District, for their contributions to the Great Lives Series.

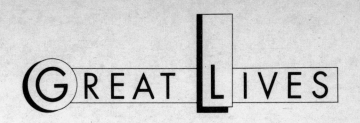

GREAT LIVES

JOHN GLENN
SPACE PIONEER

By Ann Angel

FAWCETT COLUMBINE
NEW YORK

For middle-school readers

A Fawcett Columbine Book
Published by Ballantine Books

Produced by
The Jeffrey Weiss Group, Inc.
96 Morton Street
New York, New York 10014

Library of Congress Catalog Card Number: 89-90904

ISBN: 0-449-90395-8

Cover design and illustration by Paul Davis

Manufactured in the United States of America

First Edition: February 1990

10 9 8 7 6 5 4 3 2 1

TABLE OF CONTENTS

1

Breaking the Record

THUNDER ROLLED ACROSS the heavens from Sacramento to San Diego, California. It tumbled from the sky, shaking the hills and valleys, startling curious townspeople, and rattling windows along its path. Nestled safely in the cockpit of his F8U-I Crusader jet, John Glenn heard a steady hum, followed by a whistling roar. A smile spread beneath the black mask that provided a stream of oxygen. The thirty-six-year-old, freckle-faced pilot had surpassed Mach 1, the speed of sound.

During this final practice run, Glenn, a marine pilot, became confident he would break the United States transcontinental speed record for the United States Navy. The test flight, scheduled for July 16, 1957, was only a few days away. Glenn would fly the Crusader east, from California to New York. If he did break the speed record, John Glenn's name would be written in U.S. Navy air record books, alongside those of the Wright Brothers and Charles Lindbergh. It pleased Glenn to know he would play a part in aviation history.

This is such a kick, he thought. There was no question in his mind that he would be the winner in this test of ability, daring, and speed. All his planning would pay off. Glenn knew he would happily take on "Operation Bullet" any day because, in the sky, even at great risk to himself, John Glenn knew true happiness.

Glenn's anticipation grew as the day of his flight drew closer. He focused all his attention on the smallest details as he prepared and planned. The only possible roadblock the young pilot might run into was the weather. In fact, bad weather almost postponed the historic flight.

Before dawn on the morning of the flight, Glenn and navy pilot Charlie Demmler bent over a short-wave radio, listening to last-minute weather reports. Demmler was Glenn's backup pilot and would be making the same flight, on an identical course, in another Crusader, five minutes behind Glenn. His role was to ensure that at least one pilot completed the transcontinental flight.

As the men listened to the radio, they worried about storms over the Rocky Mountains. If these didn't clear, the flights would certainly be canceled. John Glenn appreciated Demmler's friendly and cooperative attitude as they waited. But the competitive Glenn also saw Demmler as a challenger who could steal his thunder should he beat Glenn's

2

speed. Both men were keenly aware that the pilot who broke the speed record would receive national attention, as well as increased prestige within the military. Glenn did not want to hold the record for only a few short minutes. He wanted to win, and had confidence he would do so.

The excited pilots joked between themselves as they waited for the storms across the United States to subside.

"If you could manage to contract some mild disease or break a leg or something, I'd appreciate it very much," Demmler said cheerfully.

Glenn chuckled, relieved that Charlie could break the tension, and replied, "I've spoken to the ground crews and they have orders not to put any ammo in your guns. Somewhere over Pittsburgh you may get me in your sights and the temptation would be too great."

By two in the morning the weather had cleared. Relieved, Glenn and Demmler headed off for some sleep.

The morning of July 16 dawned clear and warm. John Glenn stood on the tarmac, hands on his hips and a smile spread across his handsome face. He stood almost six feet tall, with a thinning red crew-cut, and green sparkling eyes. The solid, healthy man with all-American boyish good looks was dressed for his flight in a one-piece flight suit. He breathed the warm, morning air deeply. It was going to be a perfect day for this challenging flight. The sun's first light streamed across the runway, gleaming against the waiting fighter jet. The sleek, slope-winged Crusader, fueled and ready, stood apart. The plane represented the state of the art in contemporary aircraft design.

Glenn had awakened at four A.M. Though his flight wasn't scheduled for two more hours, Glenn had been too keyed up to feel tired. Instead he entered the hangar and checked with the ground crew. The whine of airborne jets pierced the background as Glenn talked to the men. The thick smell of oil hung in the air. The restless pilot breathed deeply. Time seemed to have slowed to a nerve-racking crawl.

John Glenn looked forward eagerly to this hazardous flight. This was an opportunity to venture to the edge of speed and return in triumph. Only a few short years before, pilots thought that it was impossible to surpass 1,100 feet per second, or 750 miles per hour, the speed of sound. Indeed, the first men to try had lost control of their aircraft and crashed. Now pilots knew it was possible, but dangerous. As jets reached Mach 1, they shook and pitched so violently that only the most practiced and composed pilot could survive. The surprising aspect of passing Mach 1 was that once the pilot had done so, the flight turned calm, as the jet flew effortlessly through a sky with little turbulence.

The high speeds did put a tremendous amount of stress and pressure on a jet, though. John Glenn was going to pass Mach 1 for long stretches of time in order to break the record. He was about to put himself and the Crusader through the ultimate endurance test. At the speeds Glenn would maintain

The Bettmann Archive

Major John H. Glenn stepping out of the cockpit of the F8U–I jet fighter Crusader in which he rocketed across the nation in record time. On July 16, 1957, he flew from Los Angeles to New York City in 3 hours, 23 minutes and 8 seconds, surpassing the speed of sound and flying at speeds ranging up to 1,015 miles per hour. It was, he said, "less trouble than driving a car down the highway."

while in flight, there was little chance of survival if anything malfunctioned or if he made a poor decision.

In fact, John Glenn, like most flight test pilots, had stood at the gravesides of many fellow pilots. All of them had been friends, and none of them had thought he would ever make a wrong choice or go over the edge of daring. But for Glenn the possibility of defeat, or even death, only made the challenge more exciting. He believed he would make the right decisions in critical situations. He was confident that he would remain cool and calculating in the face of danger. Glenn had fought in two wars and gone through years of test flights. In the process he had become a skilled pilot who had pulled himself out of the most heart-stopping dangers. He was certain he would do so again. The test pilots called this "pushing the edge of the envelope," and they thrilled at any opportunity to do so.

At six A.M. John Glenn, dressed in his flight suit and wearing a radio headset, climbed into the cockpit of the waiting Crusader. His engines kicked in, then whined as the fighter plane taxied down the runway. He could feel his heart beating, blood throbbing in his head as he gained speed. His ears were filled with static and voices from the control tower. He had been cleared for takeoff. Gripping the control stick, watching the dials, Glenn felt the metal giant leave the ground. His head was pushed back as the jet shot upward, higher and higher, faster and faster.

Glenn leveled the Crusader off at 50,000 feet,

then shifted his attention to the many gauges before him. They told Glenn his altitude and speed, fuel levels and engine temperatures. They told him where he was and where he was heading. If Glenn deviated even slightly from the course across the widest section of the United States, from California to New York, it would add miles to the journey and slow him down. Every three and one-half minutes Glenn planned to communicate vital statistics with a radio checkpoint. At the same time he was constantly referring to his navigational charts, switching the toggles on his gauges and dials, flipping levers to control the air inside the tiny cockpit, and maintaining air speed.

Glenn could see the white vapor trail behind his supersonic jet fighter. Above him, the pale blue sky seemed to form a canopy. Below, Glenn saw dense white and gray clouds blanketing the country. Occasionally, through a break in the clouds, he could see a bit of river or the brown and tan patterns of plowed land. Peaks of the highest mountains jutted out from the thick clouds.

He was content as he flew across the western part of the country. His ride was smooth and serene. The marine pilot's satisfaction was well earned. He had fought hard to be where he was. This was a navy test flight. The Crusader was a navy jet fighter. And, although Glenn had flown the Crusader through some of its first handling and speed tests at Patuxent River, Maryland, it was expected that any record-breaking tests should be done by a navy pilot, not a marine such as Glenn.

This particular air test was intended to determine the Crusader's long-distance high-stress abilities. But navy administrators and John Glenn both knew the flight could end up in the record books. That meant publicity, the kind of publicity welcomed by any of the armed services branches. So it was no surprise that the navy wanted a navy pilot. But Glenn wanted the flight badly, and when this pilot wanted something, he usually won it through hard work and perseverance.

Determined and persistent, Glenn asked his navy and marine bosses to let him test the Crusader. Then he pestered them to let him make this speed test run. This pestering is considered the sign of a good man in the marines. Only those marines who master this skill find themselves with choice assignments. John Glenn was considered a master at it.

Glenn's persistence paid off. He was picked as first-choice pilot for the navy project even though he was a marine. In a bow to the navy, Demmler was made backup pilot. But John Glenn was the pilot who mapped the course and planned the test.

Long into the nights and throughout the days leading up to the test, Glenn calculated and figured. He measured and charted. He planned to the smallest detail. He organized three midair refuelings and decided their locations. He studied the plane's projected capabilities and limitations. He figured that the Crusader would travel 150 to 175 miles per hour faster than a .45-caliber bullet. He nicknamed the flight "Project Bullet."

At refueling, Glenn figured, he would have to

drop 25,000 feet and slow down. Midair refueling took a considerable amount of skill. The Crusader would descend and come up behind a fuel tanker plane. Then it would hook its probe up to the tanker's fuel hose through a funnel-type attachment called the *drogue*. Fuel would be transferred. Then the Crusader would back away from the tanker, the probe would retract, and the Crusader would regain speed.

Glenn had practiced this sensitive airborne maneuver many times. Still, now that he was doing it for real, the tension increased. If all went well, refueling would take about seven minutes. If things didn't go well, time would be lost, or, worse, refueling would not be completed. The first refueling, over Albuquerque, New Mexico, went well. However, Demmler didn't have as much luck. As he tried to maneuver his fighter into the correct position, Demmler's Crusader hit the tanker's drogue hard, bending both his probe and the drogue. Demmler was forced to land.

Glenn picked up speed between his second and third refuelings. He could feel the excitement sweep over him as he realized he was going to break the cross-country speed record. But that feeling was soon replaced with uneasiness. As Glenn swooped down below the thick clouds over Indiana to meet up with the tanker for the third refueling, the other aircraft was nowhere to be seen. Radio contact indicated that the plane was actually about five miles farther east. Glenn caught up and refueled. As he sped on his way, Glenn heard excited chatter over the radio waves — the ground crews were telling him he was going to make it!

Every three and one-half minutes, Glenn checked his navigation charts. As close as he was to breaking the record, he knew that if he went off course, even slightly, he could fall behind the record-breaking pace. He decided he needed to make up some time, and increased his speed. As the needle closed in on the Mach 1 mark, the Crusader shook and pitched. Glenn did all he could to keep a steady hand on the controls as he was bounced around in his seat. He heard a steady hum, then a whistling roar. The Crusader's violent pitching slowed, then stopped. Glenn was now rocketing across America's heartland faster than the speed of sound, faster than the proverbial speeding bullet.

His flight had left a trail of supersonic booms across the Midwest. The sleek, silver jet with the sloped wings flew over Glenn's hometown of New Concord, Ohio, at 1.3 times the speed of sound. To Glenn's parents and childhood friends, the "drag boom" that shook the Ohio hills and village streets sounded like an explosion. In fact, his excited parents and their neighbors were following his progress through reports on radio and television. They had even stood outside in their yards waiting for him to pass over. When the earth shuddered, one of the spectators said to Mrs. Glenn, "Johnny dropped a bomb! Johnny dropped a bomb!"

Meanwhile, as Glenn crossed the Ohio River he could see the green Pennsylvania meadows speeding away far below. Coming up quickly was Pittsburgh, where the snaking black line of the Ohio joined the Allegheny River. In Pittsburgh, the supersonic shock waves broke windows on the ground. On the last segment of his journey, as Glenn flew over Boston, he was ordered to slow down. Military personnel in Boston didn't want any broken windows.

Three hours, twenty-three minutes, and eight-point-four seconds after takeoff, John Glenn's transcontinental journey ended in a smooth landing at Floyd Bennett Field in New York City. He had broken the old record by twenty-one minutes. His average speed of 726 miles per hour far surpassed the previous best of 670 miles per hour.

As Glenn climbed down from the cockpit of the fighter, he was surprised to see a crowd gathered to welcome him. Certainly, he had expected some recognition from his superiors in the military. But he hadn't realized that the public impact would be so great. Schoolchildren and adults, even whole families, had caught the excitement of breaking this speed record and wanted to share in Glenn's achievement. They created a mood of celebration at the airfield. As Glenn looked over the crowd, he saw members of the military and members of the press. He also noticed small children waving American flags. As a marine band struck up the first notes of the national anthem, military officers saluted, and men, women, and children cheered.

Glenn's wife, Annie, and his two children, John David (called David) and Carolyn, had watched news accounts of the flight from a New York City hotel room before journeying out to Floyd Bennett Field. They were the first to greet the happy marine pilot who now held the new navy speed record. As reporters and TV crews jostled one another for a close-up of this peacetime hero, Glenn pulled from his pocket a pin in the shape of a cat for Carolyn and a Boy Scout knife for David. He had also carried a letter of greeting from the mayor of Los Angeles, California, to the mayor of New York.

Later, at ceremonies in his hometown, Marine Lieutenant John Herschel Glenn, Jr., was awarded his fifth Distinguished Flying Cross. In a speech reported across the nation, he said, "This thing has been a team effort all the way through. When I was brand new in this business, just out of flight school, I was told by a senior marine officer, 'When you wear this uniform, your reputation is based on dead men's deeds, so appreciate it!'" Recognizing the many brave pilots who had gone before him, the many who had lost their lives, Glenn added, "This also applies a great deal to aviation right now. . . . We certainly couldn't have done all this on our own."

The tall pilot, handsome in his dress blues, who had set out to break the speed record and succeeded, wouldn't dream of taking the glory of his success alone. He was a team player. Indeed, his eagerness to acknowledge the efforts of others had been noted when he came home a hero from World War II and the Korean War. From the very beginning, John Glenn knew the importance of cooperation.

But he was also a man who, when presented with a challenge, determinedly set out to overcome it. Accustomed to facing overwhelming odds, he refused to back down. This character trait would open opportunities for him that most other people would shy away from. It would take him into the sky and beyond, and, later in his life, into the political arena. His transcontinental air-speed record was just the beginning. Glenn was soon to become the most famous and charismatic astronaut in the world.

2

Growing Up in the Heartland

BORN JULY 18, 1921, in Cambridge, Ohio, John Herschel Glenn, Jr., was a nine-pound bundle of red hair and smiles. His mother, Clara Sproat Glenn, was a beautiful Irish blonde. She quit her job as an elementary-school teacher to raise the little boy known by friends and family as Bud. She often told the young boy, "Each person is placed on earth for a mission that he or she is obliged to fulfill for the glory of God." It was a message her son would never forget.

Bud's father, John Herschel Glenn, Sr., was a third-generation Ohioan of Scottish descent. The burly man who believed in hard work taught his son through example. He was a kind but strict father who rarely raised his voice. A few years after John's birth, the Glenns adopted an infant girl named Jean.

New Concord, Ohio, where Glenn was raised, is located in the heartland of America. It sits in a valley, hidden by rolling farm hills, filled with streams and ponds, in the center of Ohio about 100 miles southeast of Columbus. It is a tiny, clean community whose claim to fame is that this is where John Glenn grew up, went to school, and married his childhood sweetheart, Anna Castor. No longer than three city blocks, the main street boasts a grocery store, library, a few churches, and the plumbing and heating store Glenn's father owned and operated.

New Concord is a religious community, full of pride and American promise, where the people work the earth mining for coal, or raise dairy cows and sheep. Many farm their parents' land, raise their own children, and spend their lives there. It is a town where people learn to set their sights high and make their dreams come true. John Herschel Glenn, Jr., spent a happy childhood in New Concord, growing into a patriotic, religious, proud, and determined American. His parents built a supportive foundation on which to build dreams. They taught him to set his sights high and challenge himself wherever and whenever possible.

Meanwhile, all of America was facing a challenge. The country was just climbing out of a brief economic depression following World War I, which had lasted from 1914 to 1918. There weren't enough jobs for all the men who were coming home from the war overseas. The end of the war also meant that those people who had been working in factories to produce military supplies were out of work. No one thought there was any need to continue producing military materials because most Americans believed they had just suffered through "the war to end all wars." It had been devastating and brutal, ravaging most of Europe. Most American servicemen returned from the war hoping to rebuild their families and their lives, only to find that jobs were scarce and money was hard to come by.

The residents of New Concord were more fortunate than most. The Ohio coal mines were producing, so people had jobs. Nearly everyone had enough money to feed and clothe their families. The Glenns felt themselves even more fortunate because, with the senior Glenn's thriving plumbing and heating business, they were more well off than most. They shared with their neighbors and maintained close friendships.

Once a month, on Sundays, the Glenn family met with about five other families for a pot-luck supper. The children always attended. When John Glenn, Jr., was not quite four, he played at one of these gatherings with a tiny brunette girl named Anna Castor. The pretty, brown-eyed girl and the strong, green-eyed boy soon became the best of playmates. When they were old enough to attend school, the two often went to birthday parties together and paired off to work on school projects. This friendship would grow into something more lasting and loving. John Glenn, Jr., and Anna Castor would grow up and marry each other.

But at the age of five, marriage was the furthest

thing from the mind of John Glenn, Jr. The senior Glenn recalled his son's childhood as a time of dreams and fantasizing about flight. He returned home many summer evenings to find young John circling the backyard with a friend. "They'd spread their arms out like wings and go *zzzoooommm* as they ran around, dipping their arms as they banked for a turn."

This was not all. Eight-year-old John and a cousin, Bob Thompson, often spent long hours whittling balsa wood and gluing together models of World War I biplanes. The assembly of the double-winged planes, called Jennies and Spads, demanded patience and skill, but to the boys they were well worth the effort. They decorated their rooms with the finished airplanes.

Aviation, not quite thirty years old, was only in its infancy, but Glenn was hooked. He loved to watch the canvas-covered, wooden biplanes produced in the twenties as they took off and landed at a nearby airfield in Columbus, Ohio. Glenn had decided he wanted to grow up and fly.

Whether he was thinking about planes, playing with friends, or in school, John Glenn's childhood was happy and carefree. Hot and lazy summer days were spent at the Crooked Creek swimming hole, or, as he grew older, playing pickup softball in one of the many fields near the Glenns' white clapboard house. Even in the early days of spring, the sturdy redhead sported sun freckles from long hours outside.

On fall days, as maple and oak leaves turned

crimson and orange and the breezes cooled the meadows, the young boy's attention turned to his classes. A student who enjoyed school, John always received good grades. Sometimes, as he leaned over his school papers, Glenn would pause and look skyward as a plane buzzed overhead, but he would return quickly to the task before him.

A self-confident boy, John made friends quickly and easily. Throughout grade school and into high school, class pictures showed a handsome youth. Usually in the center of the front row, Glenn would be dressed in a white shirt and tie, a straight smile across his face. His eyes sparkled with interest and delight.

At New Concord High School, John played basketball, tennis, and football, and Annie watched from the bleachers. Friends joked that while Glenn often demonstrated his passion for speed driving his 1929 red roadster through the streets of New Concord, he was not as quick on the playing field.

"John wasn't a great athlete," recalled Johnny Hadden, a former teammate, "but a fine team player . . . great for morale."

Glenn was also known and liked for the funny stories he told, which broke the tension during crucial games. His coach felt he was a stabilizing factor and usually sent the redhead into football games as the starting center. He also played linebacker and in 1938 was the leading placekicker on the team. Although Glenn wasn't fleet-footed, he usually outscored his teammates on the physical tests the coach gave players. He was considered a "quality boy" who could endure any kind of roughhousing or sporting challenge. He graduated with varsity letters in each of the three sports he played: football, tennis, and basketball.

John Glenn liked to be involved and busy. He reported for his school paper, *The Maroon and White Newslite*. He played trumpet in the school band, and sang in the church choir.

Glenn was also fascinated with things mechanical and enjoyed the thrill of a fast ride. His love of speed was notable even then, when he and his friends cruised the tiny town's narrow cobblestone and dirt streets. One day young John and his friends drove Glenn's Chevy roadster through the small town, past Main Street, south to one of the county's two wooden bridges. The bridge, wide enough for only one car, had warped and buckled until it looked like a launch ramp. Glenn revved the motor as his friends shouted encouragement. He shifted into gear and popped the roadster's clutch, shooting the bridge at breakneck speed. As the car soared over the crest of the bridge, Glenn's eyes widened in horror when he saw an oncoming car. Glenn swerved with force and narrowly missed the shocked driver. This cured the young man of racing over the bridge, but it didn't stop him from cruising the county's highways at fast speeds. It took another mishap before the teen gave that up.

Recalling that second incident, the senior Glenn reported that young John returned home after an afternoon with his friends, filled with remorse, to report that he'd burned out the car's bearings while cruising the highways with his buddies. John, Sr., took away his son's driving privileges for thirty days and made him earn the amount needed to repair the car. Later, Mr. Glenn admitted he was surprised that the dejected teen-ager hadn't made a single plea for the car keys. It proved, he said, that his son had respect for discipline.

In high school, aviation was still on John Glenn's mind. He had been cultivating a deep and growing secret dream: He was thinking about becoming a pilot. But his father hoped the young man would follow him into the plumbing and heating business. The elder Glenn loved to have his young son help out with the business after school and on weekends. As in so many homes where a father hopes a son shares his dream, dinner-table talk often centered on the day's activities at work. As his father looked to his son for a hint of interest in the business, he would talk about the future. The younger Glenn listened closely and politely, pushing away thoughts of aviation. He had time to decide.

In 1938, with the seventeen-year-old Glenn in his senior year, his thoughts turned more strongly to college and career. He knew that flying was a good bet for the future because it was the most convenient and efficient method of travel. In addition, the country's military leaders understood that aviation would give the United States much-needed strength should there ever be another war. These leaders, with an eye on the building tensions in Europe, suspected that another war would occur in the near future.

Even at home, things were moving at a faster pace, mostly because of recent technological improvements. Industrial mills were busy producing the raw materials necessary for manufacturing. Farms were producing better crops with the help of motorized tractors. Trucks and trains were hauling the goods farther across the country's highways and railroads. Ships filled American ports, loading and unloading goods and foods. In Ohio, coal was being mined as quickly and efficiently as possible because industry depended on coal for fuel. More people were able to travel at greater speeds in improved automobiles, trains, and planes. The world was becoming a smaller place and young people were dreaming bigger dreams.

The commercial-airline industry was about to become a reality. Commercial planes now made of lightweight metal bodies were being mass-produced. Businesspeople realized that airplanes could be an effective method of transportation for the general public. Someone would be needed to pilot them. There was talk of pilot training, and the talk excited young John Glenn. What a way to see the world! he thought. That was something he could love to do forever.

Glenn and Annie made plans to attend Muskingum College, a group of red-brick buildings located on a hill above New Concord. Annie was going to study education. John intended to learn all he could about engineering. He wanted to be part of America's growing productivity. He dreamed of being a commercial pilot.

3

Rumors of War

JOHN GLENN OPENED the door of the "Ohio Valley Dairy" and was greeted by the familiar sounds of clattering dishes, boisterous teen voices, and jukebox music. He focused on a group of curly haired girls, who looked to be in their late teens, huddled at a table. Annie Castor, sitting in the center of the group, told the girls she'd see them later and joined Glenn at a corner table.

The busy diner, the only hangout for Muskingum College and New Concord High School students, was teeming with local couples. Young girls wearing pleated, knee-length skirts, cardigan sweaters, and saddle shoes swooped into place next to boys in wide-legged, pleated trousers, bow ties, and letter sweaters. Another nickel in the jukebox offered the fast rhythms and upbeat sounds of the Andrews Sisters or Glenn Miller and his orchestra.

Annie dipped her spoon into the chocolate ice cream she loved. John, freckle-faced and tan from his seventh summer as a YMCA lifeguard, sat across from his steady companion and finished the remains of a hot-fudge sundae. He talked excitedly about class schedules and books. Glenn had enjoyed his summer in the sun, but he was ready to return to school.

It was September 1939, and the two had just started college. Called "townies" because they lived at home, John and Annie would ride together up New Concord's hills to the small group of red-brick buildings beside the small Muskingum College lake.

Glenn and his friends saw college as the opportunity to make new beginnings, to make things happen. John Glenn's dreams had changed little since those early days when, as a four-year-old, he'd raised his arms and "flown" around the backyard. He planned a career as a commercial pilot. Now he talked to Annie about a civilian pilot program offered in nearby New Philadelphia, Ohio. As an underclassman, he was too young to enroll in the program, but he had every intention of joining as soon as he was eligible.

John Glenn didn't plan to become an astronaut. In fact, the idea would have seemed crazy in 1939. Airplanes had only been a reality since early in the century. The first jet had only just been developed in Germany. It was a prototype, or test model, considered experimental and dangerous. The new jet, a marked improvement over propeller-driven planes, offered hope for faster air travel and a stronger military defense. Meanwhile, only a few insightful minds looked beyond the blue sky to the stars and moon as possible destinations. Most of these creative geniuses kept their seemingly absurd dreams to themselves.

John Glenn kept his dreams on a realistic and attainable level. Like many other Americans, he realized that the United States might very well be drawn into another war. The civilian pilot program could give Glenn the edge he would need to become a fighter pilot if war did indeed break out. Glenn also considered military pilot training, since that could serve as the entry he'd need into a commercial pilot's life. Decisions Glenn was making then would fall neatly into the astronaut program when the time came. In the meantime, despite his father's growing impatience at the very mention of flying, being a commercial pilot was the life Glenn wanted. He knew the tiny coal town of New Concord didn't offer the opportunities he wanted. Glenn needed to go out into the world.

On September 1, 1939, Germany, under the leadership of dictator Adolf Hitler, invaded Poland. France and Great Britain, seeing a threat to their territories and wanting to put a stop to German aggression, declared war against Germany. U.S. President Franklin D. Roosevelt said the United States would stick to its policy of neutrality. Glenn and many others doubted that would remain possible for very long.

The eighteen-year-old Glenn debated the issue of

United States neutrality with the Muskingum College debating club. But it seemed silly to burden Annie and his friends with his concerns. Instead, Glenn turned his attention to his life in Ohio. He thought about joining organizations and clubs, and of upcoming dances and social events in the community.

Muskingum County in 1939 was a "dry" county — no alcohol was sold. This, together with a strong conservative and religious influence, affected social events in the community as well as life at the college. Cigarette smoking was banned. A student caught smoking off campus was suspended as quickly as a student caught on campus. Out-of-towners were not allowed to drive. Strict curfews were enforced. Although the men's dormitory posted no curfews, the curfew for women was ten P.M. on weeknights and eleven P.M. on weekends. There were no fraternities on campus, but there were social clubs.

Glenn fit in well on campus. He didn't drink or smoke, and his reputation as a good team player with courage and stamina followed him from his high school playing days. As he settled into college life, Glenn joined an athletic social club called the Stags, considered the "lookers and the dressers" on campus. Most club members were athletes who were more polished and gentlemanly than many of their peers. Like most of the club members, Glenn played football and quickly adopted the dress of the club, wearing high-collared striped shirts and tweed sport coats. If something interesting was happening on campus, John Glenn could be found in the middle of it.

Glenn continued to follow the news reports from Europe. Germany was invading and crushing its European neighbors. Denmark and Norway fell to Hitler's troops, followed by Belgium and Luxembourg. Within three months in early 1940, the Netherlands and finally France were added to the list of countries under German occupation. In the meantime, Italy, under the rule of Benito Mussolini, another dictator, had decided to join Germany in the fight for new territory. After Mussolini declared war on France, Italian troops attacked Yugoslavia and Greece. Glenn talked often with his friends about the possibility of United States involvement. It was clear to many that Europe needed help.

More and more the nineteen-year-old members of the Stags discussed their views and beliefs. If the United States was drawn into the conflict, every one of them would be called upon to fight to protect their freedoms: the freedom of their families, and the freedom of the European friends of America. Patriotism was a virtue to these men. John Glenn agreed wholeheartedly. He, too, would join the armed services and support the United States.

In September 1941, at the beginning of his second year at Muskingum College, Glenn and Annie announced to their parents that they would be married after graduation. Both sets of parents were thrilled with the news. Glenn, Sr., secretly hoped this would be the end of his son's talk of flying. He hoped that young John, now twenty, would come to his senses and enter the plumbing business with him. But such hopes were dashed when John gained acceptance into the New Philadelphia, Ohio, civilian pilot training program.

John Glenn and his friends ushered in the holiday season of 1941 with some concern. New threats were forming in Asia, as rumors spread that an aggressive Japan planned to expand its dominance in the Far East. How could anyone ignore this growing threat? Glenn thought. Sooner or later, he told himself, the United States would have to enter the fight.

The country's deepest fears were realized on December 7, 1941, when three hundred sixty Japanese planes attacked the United States naval fleet and army aircraft in a series of bombing runs at Pearl Harbor, Hawaii. During the two-hour attack, Japanese planes destroyed nineteen U.S. warships. At nearby Hickam Field, more than one hundred seventy military planes were destroyed. More than 2,000 American sailors were killed, and 237 army personnel lost their lives. Many more would be changed forever, as the United States declared war on Japan.

December 8 found millions of Americans glued to their radios, John Glenn among them. He listened intently as President Roosevelt called the previous day's destruction "a day that will live in infamy." For the next three days, Glenn heard news reports that indicated the United States was going to join the Allied forces, including Great Britain, France, and the Netherlands, in a large-scale war for survival.

On December 11, Glenn learned that Germany and Italy had joined Japan in declaring war on the United States. The U.S. Congress immediately declared war on Germany and Italy, too. Glenn turned off the radio. He needed to talk to Annie and his parents. If the United States was at risk, he saw no alternative — he had to join the armed forces and fight to save the country.

John Glenn left Muskingum College in the spring of 1942 to join the Navy Air Corps. Glenn's parents admitted they were worried about their twenty-one-year-old son's decision. The senior Glenn had enough experience to understand the dangers of flying. A veteran of World War I, he knew many soldiers never returned home. "It was like taking him out and burying him," said the elder man.

But it was an era of patriotism and pride, and John Glenn knew his country needed him. He said loving good-byes to his family, promising to return after basic training to marry Annie, then left for Corpus Christi, Texas. There, in heat so intense it seemed to blow from burning engines, Glenn learned to fly large, multi-engine seaplanes used for finding submarines. The handsome seaman had no intention of becoming a career officer. But the self-discipline and order of military training came easily to Glenn, who, by his very nature, was intent on overcoming challenges.

Glenn worked hard to understand the engineering principles necessary for him to graduate from flight school. The work was difficult, so Glenn studied that much harder. Determined to be the best, he made the additional effort necessary to excel. When he wasn't studying, he was putting in extra flying time.

While some recruits complained that they wanted to fly the "hot" fighter planes, Glenn was rather pleased to be assigned to the big planes, similar in size and handling to commercial planes. They were nicknamed "P-boats" because they looked like the patrol boats then used by the navy.

While in training, Glenn befriended Tom Miller, a man similar in nature to himself. Both had grown up in small towns. Both men attended church regularly and often spent the little free time they had attending Corpus Christi high school football and basketball games. Whenever they could, the two men would scrounge up extra flight time purely because they loved their time up in the air. Both Glenn and Miller had similar postwar plans, which included a life in the sky. These plans didn't include a life in the military. Ironically, both would ultimately become career officers.

All future plans changed dramatically the day Glenn found his name along with Miller's on a notice listing those men who qualified for promotions as officers in the marines. The curious Glenn talked Miller into attending an informational meeting. The marine recruiter looked out at the sea of innocent eyes and said, "We don't think you're good enough to be one of us."

Not good enough! Glenn couldn't believe it. This was a challenge if he'd ever heard one. He signed up on the spot and convinced Miller to do the same.

After his training was behind him, John Glenn returned home to carry out his promise to Annie. On April 6, 1943, the young marine lieutenant, dressed in a navy blue military jacket, wearing silver pilot's wings above his heart, and Anna Margaret Castor, wearing a tea-length ivory dress and rose hat with rose trim, were married in a double-ring ceremony in the United Presbyterian Church in New Concord, Ohio. After a small reception, the young couple left for the air base at Cherry Point, North Carolina, where Glenn had just been assigned. Less than a year later, Glenn received his orders to go overseas. Although Annie would return to New Concord, John Glenn would never return to his hometown for more than a short visit. The larger world had captured him. His first stop there was the center of World War II.

4

The Flying Hero

MANY MARINES FOUND that to qualify for war duty they had to put in a series of training efforts in tiny little towns and villages scattered across the United States. They were disappointed because they had longed to support the United States war effort at the front. The bored men complained loudly that they'd expected to fight for democracy, not sleep away the war. John Glenn's first orders were only slightly less disappointing. At least, he thought, he'd have the opportunity to fly.

Glenn's first stop, in May 1943, was in the emerald hills of North Carolina, where he was to train as a fighter pilot on the Corsair, a propeller-driven fighter with a clear, domed canopy. In training, the twenty-one-year-old pilot learned to rely on his fellow fliers and team effort.

Fighter pilots like to talk about "pushing the edge

of the envelope." This refers to flying a plane to the limits of endurance and speed, then returning safely. It was important to understand, as John Glenn did, that this was not an invitation to practice daredevil tactics. Rather, the handsome pilot with the red crewcut and freckles learned that a clear eye on his target and an accurate hand on the controls could mean a life saved and a successful run. Sloppiness caused defeat and death. Glenn also learned to rely on his wingman when flying missions. The wingman is the pilot who flies on the left or right of the central plane in a group of bombers. These pilots cover the center plane. Sometimes, this means firing at trucks and tanks on the ground. Sometimes it means firing at enemy planes. Often, this fighting is at close range, and it isn't without risks.

In February 1944, Glenn was assigned to protect a submarine base located on the island of Midway, in the Pacific Ocean southwest of Hawaii. However, Glenn's new home was no lush, tropical paradise. Rather, Midway was one of a group of flat and sandy islands cooled by dry sea breezes. The coral sands covering the floor of the islands produced little but the scruffiest vegetation. As far as he could see, tiny dust storms blew around sparse groupings of cocoa palms and breadfruit trees. The flat land seemed to spread out forever. The relentless sun beat down on the marines day after day, baking them in its dry heat. Days on this Pacific retreat were filled with tedium, broken only by an occasional bombing mission.

Glenn soon discovered that the war was being won at a terrible cost to human life. "I can remember," he recalled, "walking around a beach on Tarawa and seeing what looked like pieces of petrified flesh. Starting up my engines once, I saw exhaust stir up skulls and bones out of the sand."

Tarawa is one of a group of islands called the Marshall Islands, which lie just south of Midway. Halfway between the United States and Japan, they had been controlled by the Japanese until shortly before U.S. troops captured the two northernmost islands in the group of twenty-eight. Tiny as these dusty islands were, they were terribly important to the United States war effort. If Japan could regain control there, then push up and gain control of Midway, Japanese troops would easily be able to attack the United States mainland!

It was decided that heavy bombing to destroy the enemy's equipment and artillery was necessary to keep Japanese forces from overtaking the area. This was now Glenn's job. He flew with a group of pilots who referred to themselves as the "Ready Teddy" squadron, a name Glenn had thought up on his arrival. He also created the squadron logo. The scrambling teddy bear, parachute pack streaming out from behind, waved from the silver bodies of fighter planes lining the runway.

Loaded down with three 1,000-pound bombs, Glenn, along with at least one partner, would fly in low over Japanese artillery sites, motor pools, and military camps. As he gained experience, he became an expert at wiping out enemy positions with fire bombs. Glenn was only pleased with missions in which all his bombs were on target. He gained a reputation as a dependable flier who used his solid knowledge and experience to accomplish his missions. He was truly a perfectionist and never left anything to chance. In truth, he would have preferred more air-to-air combat, but he performed whatever task his superiors deemed necessary.

Glenn's squadron included Tom Miller, who had become a close friend during training. Miller believed Glenn to be one of the best pilots in his squadron. The other pilots gained an immediate respect for Glenn's perfectionist attitude toward his bombing missions. In fact, Glenn quickly became the wingman of choice.

The Ready Teddys were often riddled with machine-gun fire and shelled by larger bombs as they flew. Glenn would just narrow his focus on his targets and zoom in as close as possible. After hitting his target, he would pull up sharply and return to base. As he looked back, he could see burning buildings, jeeps, and trucks surrounded by scorched grass and trees. Glenn thought of this fighting as a test of his abilities. It was exciting and challenging. Glenn's colleagues admired him for his courage, but there was no getting around the fact that war included death. At times, this haunted the young man.

Death took on a more personal meaning on July 10, 1944. Tanned and rugged from his months on the base, John Glenn boarded his silver Corsair to make a bombing run on the Japanese island of Maloelap. Glenn was to be a lead pilot along with his close friend, Tom Miller. They were joined by two wingmen. Glenn's was a young lieutenant and good friend, Monte Goodman. The pilots took off into the blue Pacific sky and prepared for their assigned roles. Glenn stared intently over the water dotted with tiny brown islands. As the pilots found their targets, Glenn joined the others in a rapid dive. He dropped his bombs, reeled up toward the sun to escape enemy fire, and made his way toward the squad's planned rendezvous point.

The pilots had made these moves together many times. Usually, the maneuvers went smoothly. The trick was to "drop your load," roll away from anti-aircraft fire, and regroup on the way back to base. Glenn carried out the procedure perfectly. His tense shoulders relaxed and he sat back, hands on the controls, ready to make the easy ride back to base.

It was then that he heard a voice over the radio. "Who was that who went into the water?" called a pilot. Glenn looked for his own wingman. He didn't see Goodman. He craned his neck as far back as he could see. He searched the endless sky and looked below for signs of a dropping parachute. He searched for some hope that his wingman was okay. There was no sign of Goodman. He called over his radio, "Red Two, are you aboard? Red Two, where are you?"

The airwaves remained silent, except for Glenn's own voice. Glenn banked hard to the right and flew over the island they had just bombed. He couldn't take his eyes off the dark, floating shape he finally saw. He stared, disbelieving at the chilling sight.

"All we could see," he recalled, "was an oil slick. That's all we ever found."

The quiet men returned to the base, where a pall fell over the squadron. Each felt the loss deeply. John Glenn was upset, his face a stern mask as he climbed down from the cockpit. If there were tears, they were shed alone because John Glenn knew the code. There was no reason to upset the men any more than necessary; news of the loss would upset them enough. He felt a responsibility to his friend and wingman, but he also felt a responsibility to the men who would fly the next mission. Except for the overwhelming silence that spread across the base, there was no outward display of grief. Each man in his own way dealt with the loss of a good friend and fellow pilot. They also worked to maintain the morale of the unit. John Glenn would never forget the face of death. It made him more careful in his accuracy, and it made him more determined to win the war.

By the time the Allies triumphed and the war ended on August 14, 1945, Glenn had flown fifty-nine hazardous missions, winning four Distinguished Flying Crosses and fifteen Air Medals. Many of those missions were flown because Glenn had volunteered, but many were undertaken because a fellow pilot had requested Glenn's support. The men agreed that if there were only one chance to succeed at any given mission, whether they were digging a ditch or bombing a target, John Glenn was the man to ask. He never missed. And he never refused to take part.

In September 1945, the twenty-four-year-old war hero returned home filled with victory. He and Annie shared a loving reunion in New Concord with their parents. In December, their first child was born, a son named John David. But all too soon, another war would beckon. John Glenn would soon return to battle to fight the Korean War, and again he would bring with him the determination to win, or die trying.

5

MIG-Mad Marine

THE BITTER WINDS of the winter monsoon stung John Glenn's face and whipped his bare hands as he stared over the Korean landscape on a frigid February day in 1953. Glenn hunched his shoulders, buried his chin in the collar of his heavy parka, and jammed his hands deep inside his pockets. He stared up at the rounded, snow-covered mountain peaks jutting from the horizon. Then he walked back toward a low row of buildings.

Sometimes, the howling winds made the Quonset huts shudder. Inside, mechanics and crew members working on the silent jets would stop, stand statue-still, and wait for the wailing to end. Outside, the pilots watched the horizon through squinted eyes as wind storms swirled around them. Even walking from building to building was a challenge as the wind pushed against the strongest men and the freezing cold bit red and white on exposed ears and chins.

From the safety of the building, the thirty-one-year-old pilot looked out at the slate sky as clouds coasted past. He wished he could fly that day but he knew no planes would take off. The monsoons would hold them to the ground.

In the sky, above the clouds, it didn't matter what the weather was like below. Glenn loved the view from the sky. From above, the Korean foothills, dotted with trees and brush, looked like the hills of southeastern Ohio. Clouds looked like wispy white veils. The blue umbrella above was intense and clear. Looking from side to side, Glenn could always see his partners' planes. The bombers flashed silver and gray in the sun. The sky was an open invitation offering freedom, speed, and challenge to the "fly-boys." John Glenn accepted that challenge.

During the seven short years of peace since World War II, Glenn had become an expert on the newest, fastest military aircraft. He had worked at air bases around the world as a marine pilot, taking advantage of many opportunities to fly some of the sleek experimental military aircraft being designed. These fighters and bombers were used in peacetime to patrol allied and enemy coasts around the world. The silver-winged, long-tailed planes were becoming faster and more capable. Engine modifications now included after-burners. In jet engines, compressed air and burning fuel mix to produce great thrust. When after-burners were added, the fuels were re-ignited as they passed out of the engines, producing greater acceleration for the lighter aircraft.

Faster acceleration meant pilots were able to gain altitude more quickly, and maneuver more swiftly to evade ground attacks. Glenn easily adapted his skills to these fighters. He learned to fly low and quick to avoid radar in enemy territory. Many of the planes Glenn flew were newer versions of the propeller planes he had flown in World War II, such as North American Mustangs and Boeing bombers. Sometimes, Glenn flew the newest experiments in air design. These jets were faster and more maneuverable than any of the earlier planes he had flown during his first war experience.

Glenn loved every minute of this peacetime test-flying. But he had to make certain sacrifices, such as long separations from Annie and his son. In 1947, when his daughter, Carolyn, was born in Zanesville, Ohio, Glenn was flying border patrols in China. Even when he was stationed in the United States, Glenn's job often required that he stay close to base, where he lived in quarters provided by the marine corps. When time allowed, Glenn returned to his wife and children, and whenever possible, the family joined Glenn on his assignments. While Glenn was patrolling the Great Wall of China, Annie, David, and the new baby flew over to stay with him. Shortly after their return from China, the family packed off to Guam. There Glenn continued patrol duties with his family nearby. The family cherished its time together and tried to remain a close and loving group.

This closeness made it difficult for Glenn to join the conflict in Korea. In doing so, he left Annie, Carolyn, and David in the care of Annie's parents in New Concord. A war zone was no place to raise a family, Glenn thought. But he was committed to supporting the United States's effort to preserve personal freedom for itself and its allied nations. Annie understood this. And so the thirty-one-year-old marine entered the Korean War as an operations officer in charge of planning and carrying out missions.

The United States had entered the Korean War to "save the world from communism." Communism is a system based on property ownership by a community as a whole or by the state. Communist societies are characterized by Communist Party control over all political and social activity and by central planning of the economy.

Many Americans thought communism was a terrible system because, among other things, it restricted personal freedom. Citizens were often arrested for speaking out against the government. In addition, since many Communists spoke of sparking a worldwide Communist revolution, many people considered the movement a threat to world peace. On the other hand, many other people thought that communism represented the world's greatest hope for justice. In Russia, for example, the people had firmly embraced the Communist goal of equality and security for all through government ownership and strict rule. In 1917, Russia declared itself a Communist country and changed its name to the Union of Soviet Socialist Republics (USSR), or Soviet Union. By 1940, sixteen nations had come under Communist control.

That same year, the United States had promised to aid non-Communist countries that were attacked by Communist nations. The Soviet Union reacted angrily, and tension resulted between the two countries, which had been allies during World War II. Hostilities mounted during the early 1950s. The so-called "cold war" had begun.

Domestically, there was a growing fear that communism was running rampant through America's institutions. Senator Joseph R. McCarthy of Wisconsin charged that many Communists had succeeded in gaining sensitive jobs in the army and the State Department. He held a series of televised hearings in which his charges were aired. He failed to prove his accusations and was later reprimanded by the Senate, but he succeeded in creating a fearful atmosphere throughout much of the country. For example, in Hollywood, California, the country's movie capital, fear of communism ended promising careers as movie stars, writers, and directors found they would not be hired if they refused to sign anti-Communist oaths. The term "McCarthyism" is still a term often used in American politics.

The confrontation between the two systems came to a head on the Korean peninsula in northeast Asia. While South Korea maintained a democracy, North Korea had joined the Communist camp. On June 25, 1950, North Korea attempted to expand its boundaries by invading South Korea. China fought on the side of North Korea, and the Soviet Union sent aid as well.

The United Nations, an international peacekeeping organization founded after World War II, became involved. At the U.N.'s suggestion, seventeen U.N. countries sent supplies to South Korea. The United States supplied more than ninety percent of the military personnel, weapons, food, and other supplies used during what turned out to be the bloodiest conflict in history. Approximately 1,500,000 Communist troops and 580,000 U.N. and South Korean troops were killed, wounded, or reported missing. This was more than double the number of military casualties sustained during World War II. In addition, more than 1,000,000 civilians died. For three years, tanks roamed the hilly terrain of Korea, crushing trees, houses, and villagers in their wake. Bombs landed on army bases, artillery storage sheds, and villages full of old men, women, and children. Hardly a corner of Korea would be left untouched. At war's end the boundaries between North and South Korea remained almost as they had been before the war.

When he went to Korea, John Glenn hoped to fly F-86 Sabre jets, new military jets that were said to be incredibly swift and accurate. These fighters had yet to be tested in man-to-man contact against the Soviet-designed MIG-15, a small, swept-wing jet with a Rolls-Royce engine. The MIG-15 was the fastest, most maneuverable interceptor jet to date. Many said it could easily outfly any of the jets, including Sabres, manned by United Nations allies. Battles between Sabre jets and MIG's would be balanced only because U.S. pilots had more training and experience than their Chinese and North Korean counterparts.

MIG and Sabre jet pilots became skilled at dodging and skirting one another. If a pilot couldn't evade the enemy, he had no choice but to use his machine guns. These fights were called dogfights. They were deadly, but they were a true test of a pilot's ability and courage. John Glenn knew he had that ability and courage. He wanted to experience a dogfight.

At first, Glenn was assigned bombing missions, as in World War II. He flew these missions with the same bull's-eye perfection as before. Zigzagging to avoid enemy fire, he learned quickly that the mountainous hills and lush ground cover in Korea hid many enemies. Missions took on an added danger as he learned to expect enemy fire from every clump of trees.

Once, after hitting a target, Glenn made a second sweep, something he'd been warned against doing, since enemies would be better prepared for his approach. Sure enough, his plane was hit by a 90-mm shell, which blew a large hole in the tail fin and sent Glenn into a dive. As the ground rushed to meet him, Glenn pulled up on the controls. But the jagged metal surrounding the damaged rubbed against the plane's elevator. Glenn couldn't get the flipper in place, and he was sure he was facing certain death. Desperately, with every last bit of strength, he pulled his elevator control up and managed to get just enough movement out of the damaged tailpiece to force the plane out of its dive. When he finally landed, Glenn discovered the plane had 250 holes in it. But as close as he'd been to death, Glenn was fearless. Still in his flight suit, and helmet in hand, he jumped up on the wing and posed for a buddy's camera. He told everyone within earshot that that was the closest he had ever come to "buying the farm," and he grinned a wide grin. Friends were beginning to get the impression that Glenn would rather fly than eat.

But Glenn experienced losses in this war. He learned again that no matter how noble the mission or cause, personal loss was always bitter, always painful. Not all the losses ended in death. Some members of Glenn's unit ended up in enemy prison camps. A proud and brave fighter, this green-eyed man who still bore a look of youth wasn't embarrassed to acknowledge his pain. Sometimes he cried. Other times, if he thought he could help, he bore down all the more to save a fellow pilot. John Glenn always felt responsible for his squadron.

One time, on a routine bombing mission, Glenn's partner, Colonel John C. Giroudo, was shot down over enemy lines while flying at Glenn's side. From the cockpit of his own black-and-gray Corsair, Glenn could see Giroudo parachute down and land in a thicket of trees. Glenn circled and came in low, buzzing the treetops as he searched the paths and shrubs for any sign of his fellow pilot. Nothing.

Glenn flew over the area again and again, coming in low and circling up, only to repeat the pattern. By now, though, Giroudo had been taken prisoner by the Chinese. Every time they heard Glenn's plane fly over, they threw Giroudo into the brush and covered him with their own bodies. Glenn had no way of knowing that Giroudo had been captured, nor that the enemy was camouflaging his partner. But Glenn wasn't about to abandon Giroudo out there. He went over the area once more, searching and scanning. Finally, Glenn, dangerously close to running out of fuel, climbed back into the sky. In order to make it back to base, Glenn accelerated with the last of his fuel, then flamed out his engine and glided home for 108 miles. As he prepared to make a "dead stick" landing, the brave pilot radioed home to prepare a search team.

Upon landing, Glenn jumped from his plane and ran to the waiting search planes. Without a word to the ground crew, he boarded one of the craft and returned to the area where he'd seen Giroudo go down. Only when it grew dark did the determined pilot return to base, disappointed and dejected.

A little less than two years later, on the day when prisoners of war were exchanged between the warring countries, John Glenn stood with the expectant families and friends of his compatriots. He was there to greet his friend, Colonel John C. Giroudo. As the freed prisoners streamed from the idling plane, Glenn maintained his composure. Ever the cool marine pilot, he waited patiently, stiffly, for his friend. Giroudo disembarked and couldn't believe his eyes. The two men clasped each other in a bear hug, and tears finally streamed down Glenn's face.

Within four months of arriving in Korea, Glenn had flown sixty-three fighter bomber missions, earning another Distinguished Flying Cross and six air medals. Still, John Glenn wanted a taste of fighter interceptor flying. He wanted to dogfight.

There *were* dogfights in the skies. Often, a pilot, flying in the Sabre jet, would end up in deadly air-to-air combat in order to protect the larger fighter bombers. All the pilots believed these Sabres were the most interesting aircraft. They certainly received the most publicity, and their pilots were celebrated by newspapers, radio, and television, as America's fair-haired boys. And why not? They risked their lives daily in order to save the South Korean people from losing their freedom.

Finally, in June 1953, Glenn was assigned to the air force's 25th Fighter Squadron 51st Wing as an exchange pilot. He would get his chance behind the controls of the famed Sabre jet. He couldn't believe it!

But when he returned from his first few Sabre flights, John Glenn complained. He hadn't spotted a single MIG. Glenn, all keyed up for a big mission, was disappointed. He was reminded that this meant the fighter bombers were able to do their job unmolested. But after a few more flights, he complained again. In fact, he talked so frequently about dogfights and about air-to-air combat that he earned the nickname "MIG-Mad Marine."

One night, as Glenn slept, the squadron painter decorated Glenn's fighter in red and gold, the marine colors. Glenn was amused and surprised to discover "MIG-Mad Marine" painted in huge letters below the cockpit of his fighter.

Finally, on the clear, warm morning of July 12, 1953, Glenn's opportunity to fight man-to-man arrived. The monsoon blew sticky, hot winds against Glenn's skin as he walked toward the runway. Pebbles and grit stung his cheeks. Glenn didn't really mind the heat and humidity. Remembering the bitter cold and biting northern monsoons that blew through Korea in February, he saw the current weather as a relief.

Glenn took off into the blue horizon on his assigned mission. Leading the flight along the Yalu River, which separates Korea from China, he spotted two low-flying MIG's coming toward him. He called "Bounce," the signal to his wingman to join the attack, into his headset. He made a sweeping turn to position himself and came up fast behind the MIG's. When the two MIG's split up, Glenn zeroed in on one as his wingman focused on the other. Glenn opened fire, pulling up to avoid ramming the MIG's tail. He was surprised at the sight of bullets as they hit the enemy. They lit up like a thousand tiny sparks against the silver metal frame. He'd hit the MIG's fuselage and wings. At 1,000 feet, the MIG nosed over and began to spin toward the ground. The right wing and fuselage burst into flames before it hit. Glenn looked over his shoulder at the wreckage. There wasn't much to see — some scorched ground and burning metal scraps. Glenn radioed in, "Confirmed kill."

The second MIG escaped. The fighter bomber Glenn and his wingman had been commissioned to protect continued on its mission unscathed, while Glenn returned to formation. Upon returning to the base, a red star was painted on the cockpit recording Glenn's combat record. Within two weeks, it was to be joined by two more stars.

On July 16, Glenn shot down his second MIG in a hair-raising battle against sixteen enemy aircraft. "Airplanes were going in every direction," he wrote later. "The MIG I picked broke out of the general melee in a diving turn." Glenn followed and commenced firing. But the MIG pilot was skilled, and executed a number of turns that the Sabre jet couldn't follow. Glenn, in turn, executed a series of dives and turns, hoping to force the MIG to follow. Just then, Glenn's wingman swooped into position next to Glenn and fired on the MIG. It smoked, pulled up sharply, then spun to the ground.

A dizzying blur of blue sky and gray-green horizon appeared before Glenn as he pulled away from the fight. Over the headset, Glenn heard the frantic voice of his wingman, who had developed engine trouble and needed someone to protect him. Without a thought for his own safety, Glenn kept up his speed and flew circles around the slowing wingman as he tried to escape the combat area.

Against the pale blue sky, Glenn spotted six shiny-silver jets above him. He realized they were MIG's even before they swept into position and started firing on him and his injured partner. They attacked in a long string, all moving toward the two

F-86's. Glenn pulled up. Maintaining contact and passing directional information over the headset, Glenn aimed head-on toward the enemy. He fired. The MIG leader broke away. Glenn's machine gun continued to blast. Sparks flew as the bullets hit the MiG's fuselage. The smoking MIG rolled over and spiraled to the ground.

The other five MIG's continued coming at Glenn in ones and twos. Every time he spotted one coming toward him, Glenn shot off a round of fire. Each time a MIG broke off the attack it was replaced by a fresh fighter. In the turmoil, Glenn lost sight of his wingman. Glenn radioed his concern. The wingman responded that he was in the clear and had no aircraft in sight. Because Glenn's first responsibility was to protect his injured wingman, he knew he had to escape the MIG and rejoin his squadron. Glenn made a move called the split-S to gain speed, and returned to the airfield, rejoining his wingman on the way.

Upon landing, Glenn saw that the nose of his silver F-86 had been blackened by heavy firing of his machine guns. He himself was tired but pleased. He and his wingman had faced one of the most incredible battles of their careers and lived to tell about it.

Glenn later wrote about his experiences. "Needless to say, this was a rather hair-raising day," he said, "but it demonstrated the value of teamwork." No doubt this was an understatement. But Glenn's heroic deeds that day also demonstrated his ability to focus single-mindedly on a job and get it done.

Just a few days before the Koreans called an uneasy truce, on July 21, 1953, John Glenn added a third star to his aircraft when he shot down another MIG in a battle in which the last three MIG's of the war were downed.

If the war had continued, Glenn most certainly would have shot down the five enemy planes needed for a pilot to be declared an "Ace." Two short of his goal, Glenn nonetheless demonstrated he had the necessary desire, skill, experience, and courage. Reporting on his war record, the local paper said John Glenn just ran out of war. It didn't take long for Glenn to find new frontiers to conquer.

6

Pushing the Edge of the Envelope

THE SOLDIERS WHO came home from Korea were greeted as heroes. Parades were held in their honor and the country's political leaders applauded their patriotism. But they quickly put aside their uniforms, titles, and memories for civilian jobs and careers and to settle down with family and friends. Loans, made available through the G.I. Bill of Rights, gave many veterans the opportunity to buy or build homes, farms, and businesses. Many others took advantage of education and job-training benefits through the G.I. Bill. Some pilots, soldiers, and seamen who'd found careers in the military opted to sign up for peacetime duty. They were surprised when they found themselves stuck behind desks piled high with paper work.

John Glenn was one of the pilots arriving home from battle. He was greeted proudly by Annie, Carolyn, and David. As he became reacquainted with his family, he discovered their likes and dislikes. He learned through Carolyn that young girls easily become infatuated with movie stars and rock-'n'-roll singers but that no one could replace a loving father. David showed him that young boys always thought their fathers were heroes.

For a short time, the thirty-two-year-old marine pilot visited with his parents and in-laws, who had made a home for Annie and his children during the war. But their reunion was short. New Concord in 1954 just couldn't offer the life John Glenn had in mind. He still wanted to fly. But he didn't want to fly just anything. Dreams of flying commercial planes had lost their luster when Glenn compared them to his war experiences. He'd gotten a taste of "pushing the edge," and he wanted to continue. He knew he could push the edge of the envelope daily if he flew experimental aircraft.

Test pilots were some of the best pilots in the country. It took a great deal of bravery to become a test pilot. A test pilot would board a jet that embodied all the right *principles* of physics and aerodynamics, but until he reached the end of the runway, he wouldn't know if the design actually worked. The test pilot was respected for his ability to risk his life daily. Many men wanted to become test pilots, but only an elite few were ever accepted. Pilots were expected to enter the program with college degrees or the equivalent thereof. They would graduate from the program as graduate-level engineers. Many of those accepted would never graduate because the classwork was so complicated and exhausting.

The determined Glenn again made the most of his own opportunities. Despite his lack of a college degree, he made his way into the program by letting his outstanding war record speak for his accomplishments. Glenn made it into flight-test school partially because of this record, but also because of his winning attitude. His Korea-based superiors had a high regard for his ability to overcome obstacles through hard work. It didn't hurt that he had requested letters of recommendation from every superior he knew! In working to gain acceptance into the elite flight test program, Glenn planned to make a career of challenging himself as a flier. He couldn't know then that he was also taking steps to qualify for the space program, which in 1954 was only in its experimental stages.

Glenn entered flight-test school in 1954 at the Naval Test Center in Patuxent River, Maryland. There, Glenn felt at home. Overhead, planes buzzed and circled the blue sky. The smell of fuel mixed with steady breezes from the river and the salt water of Chesapeake Bay. Loudspeakers constantly droned information and orders across the tarmac.

When he wasn't flying, Glenn kept his nose in a book. As much as he wanted this opportunity, his desire didn't make the work any easier. This was a difficult and miserable time for him. Calculus wasn't just hard, it was impossible. Analytics and trigonometry, necessary to understanding the fundamental design of experimental aircraft, almost put Glenn out of the program. He was worried.

How was he to understand the principles behind a jet's performance if he didn't have the tools necessary to determine its agility and endurance? He needed to be able to comprehend the effect that the weight of artillery had on a jet's performance. He needed to be able to calculate how a jet would perform with strong tail winds or crosswinds. What would happen if a jet banked to turn in a sudden undercurrent of air? Could a jet with thin, long wings take off at a sixty-degree angle? How about seventy degrees? He would never know if he couldn't calculate the numbers, and he couldn't do that without advanced algebra, calculus, and trigonometry. He needed physics, too.

Most pilots accepted into flight school had this background. Many had college degrees in engineering. John Glenn had left Muskingum College after only two and a half years. He hadn't taken the advanced courses. In fact, compared to the other candidates for flight school, Glenn's academic credentials were slim. Schoolwork, for Glenn, was a continuous struggle. John Glenn recognized a disadvantage when he saw it. But he also recognized a challenge. It wasn't life or death, but if he didn't overcome these obstacles, the thirty-three-year-old pilot might just find himself reassigned to a desk job, or, worse, back in New Concord, running the family business. He wouldn't let either happen. John Glenn knew he belonged in the sky.

While Annie and the kids remained in New Concord, Glenn once again lived a student's life, studying and cramming, memorizing and deciphering, working doggedly to catch up. He spent long nights learning what it seemed everyone else already knew. Days were full and intense. Pilots were also expected to maintain their flight schedules. Before Glenn tackled his books in the evening, he had to fill out flight reports. John Glenn didn't let up on himself for a second. At one point, Glenn believed the lack of knowledge would overcome his struggle. But no challenge was too big, he reminded himself. After all, he'd survived two wars. Surely he could survive flight-test school. He had a reputation for being a terrific competitor. He had heard other pilots talk about how he scrambled for everything. He was proud that they recognized his persistence. Deep down, Glenn didn't want to be topped by anyone.

In August 1954, Glenn graduated. Annie and the kids were finally able to join him in his new assignment at Patuxent River as project officer of the Patuxent Armament Test Division. He was assigned to "wire out" new military aircraft. This meant that Glenn was authorized to judge the stamina, behavior, and endurance of newly designed aircraft. In other words, he risked his life to prove design engineers right or wrong. During the next two years, he tested Chance-Vought Cutlasses, the Douglas Skyray, and the F8U-I Crusader, the aircraft used to break speed records while traveling at speeds of 1,015 miles per hour in 1956. It was this record

Glenn would break in 1957 flying the Crusader across the United States.

Life at the air base was rewarding for the pilots who were sent out across Chesapeake Bay to fly aerial stunts, to perform mock dogfights, and to drop artillery on targets. Often Glenn would find himself on the Chesapeake Bay on an aircraft carrier, flying experimental aircraft. Glenn loved to shoot off the flight deck toward the blue-green sea. He would open the throttle to gain speed and altitude as quickly as possible. The jet would charge off the deck and fly out across the bay, in some cases matching speeds and altitudes pilots had originally thought only land-based jets were capable of.

There was also a special aura around the air base because of something that had happened in October 1957. Then, Glenn had been held spellbound as he watched televised reports that the Soviet Union had placed a satellite called *Sputnik I* into earth's orbit. The reporter announcing the launch spoke anxiously about the potential threat this could be to the United States. Pointing to an artist's illustration of satellites floating among stars, the reporter warned that the Russians could use the satellite to spy on the United States. The "space race" had begun, and the United States was behind.

Glenn doubted the United States was in any danger. He'd heard things around the air base indicating that the United States was working to use space technology, too. It was too bad that the Soviets had beaten the United States into space, but he suspected the Americans would get their turn. As Glenn listened, he became very interested. He wondered how long it would take to send a human into orbit. He wondered if there was a role for a pilot in space, and if he could possibly be a part of the program. Glenn decided to keep his eye on the United States's efforts to get into space. Maybe there'd be a place for him.

In the meantime, he concentrated on his work. He was good at his job. Promotions were quick and many. In fact, in 1957, they led to an administrative position that took him out of the sky and placed him behind a desk in Washington, D.C. Glenn didn't flinch or complain, but there was no question that he would rather be flying.

Glenn had been on some of the first flights of the United States's jet known as the Crusader. He knew this machine could break all existing flight speed records, and he was determined to be the pilot of any such flights. He organized his own opportunity for "Operation Bullet," the July 16, 1957, transcontinental flight that broke speed records and demonstrated the navy Crusader's stability and endurance. Glenn came up with the idea for the flight, then flew the Crusader at speeds averaging 725 miles per hour, from California to New York. He managed three midair refuelings and demonstrated that the jet could endure stress when it was pushed to maximum speeds over long periods of flight.

The hero's welcome Glenn received when he landed in New York was surprising, but nothing new to the pilot who had been welcomed home from war as a decorated military hero. It was the first time, however, that he made national news. Across the country, newspapers, radio stations, and television reporters heralded Glenn because he had risked his life to ensure that America had quality aircraft for its military.

The New York Times called him the man of the hour. Glenn's hometown paper published photos of Glenn standing proudly with his family as he was welcomed by a military band and the mayor of New York. Glenn enjoyed the attention. He posed in his flight suit, holding his helmet at his side. Although the thirty-seven-year-old pilot's red crewcut was thinning, he boasted a handsome smile and an all-American boyish charm that won nationwide admiration.

Before long, the excitement caused by Glenn's flight died down, and he was back at his desk in Washington, D.C. — but not for long. Glenn was already planning his next move. Lately, he'd been hearing rumors that the National Advisory Committee on Aeronautics, which subsequently became the National Aeronautics and Space Administration, or NASA, had moved beyond unmanned rocket experiments. The program's administrators would soon be looking for volunteers to man the nation's first space flights.

This, thought Glenn, was something to strive for. As in the past, when Glenn set his sights on something, he worked unceasingly to obtain it. Whenever the opportunity arose to test equipment related to the space program, Glenn volunteered. Often, he would sit in on conferences concerning needed improvements for the equipment. He wanted to make sure the program's administrators knew his name when the time came. Throughout 1958, he made sure he was visible to the right people.

As the year neared its close, the requirements for being an astronaut were announced by NASA officials. The applicant would need a college degree. He would have to be in the military, and his record should include flight-test experience. It certainly wouldn't hurt if the applicant had flown in combat. Because NASA administrators weren't sure what the astronaut would experience in space, the applicant had to be in the best possible physical and psychological conditions. He would undergo an intense battery of tests. This was a man who would have to endure the most difficult training of any man in military history. No one over age forty would be selected. Finally, the candidate had to be under five feet, eleven inches tall because the completed capsule allowed for only limited space.

John Glenn looked at the list of requirements. He had a few obstacles to overcome if he was to make the program. He didn't have a college degree. At 208 pounds, he was overweight, and he was almost an inch too tall. Well, he decided, it was time to get to work. The thirty-seven-year-old marine planned a rigorous training program for himself. Tom Miller, a friend since basic training and Glenn's neighbor, also became involved. "I'm going down to one sixty-seven," Glenn told him.

The training began. Every evening the two men

left the office and headed for a workout at the Officers' Club at the Pentagon, the building housing the U.S. Department of Defense. Glenn ran and swam. He lifted weights and worked on the trampoline, sweating out every extra ounce. When he reached 190 pounds, Miller told him he looked fine. He'd lost enough weight. But Glenn didn't want to take any chances. His weight continued to drop until he reached his goal of 167 pounds.

The height problem was, admittedly, a bit more difficult. Glenn walked around with twelve inches of books on his head for at least two hours every evening. Then he'd stand beside the den doorway and measure himself against a five-foot-eleven mark. His friend Miller simply shook his head in amusement and wonder. He had never seen such determination, he said, but he doubted Glenn's book idea would work. Miller was shocked when the beaming Glenn reported that they had, apparently, done the trick. Today, Glenn's height is still listed as five feet, ten and one-half inches tall.

Next, Glenn tackled the problem of his lack of a college degree. He had more than enough credits. He'd just never stayed anywhere long enough to complete an official degree program. First, Glenn had more than two years of course work at Muskingum College. He'd completed graduate-level course work at Patuxent. After World War II, he'd taken college courses at the Armed Forces Institute. Most recently, while working at the Pentagon, Glenn had taken college courses at the University of Maryland. He applied to Muskingum College to accept transfer credits and award him a degree. To Glenn's dismay, the tiny college turned him down on a residency requirement. He reapplied and was turned down again. By the time NASA began weeding out potential astronaut candidates, the worried Glenn still didn't have a degree. Just in time, the University of Maryland awarded Glenn a degree based on the credits he'd taken.

All the time Glenn was struggling to meet astronaut requirements, he continued to volunteer for every experimental program that involved the astronaut selection committee. One such experiment involved a machine that simulated the extreme forces of gravity that occur during a rocket launch. In this machine, the subject of the experiment is strapped in place and spun around at gradually increasing speeds. Glenn was wired with electrodes to monitor his breathing and heart rate. After his ride, he was also expected to report on changes his body experienced as the machine's speed increased. While spinning, Glenn reported, his body felt heavier than usual. Sometimes breathing became difficult. If he didn't focus his eyes straight ahead, he felt nauseated. After the ride, it took him a while to steady his legs.

All of his hard work was paying off. Glenn was remembered. He also met all the requirements for the program. Soon NASA would be narrowing the list of eligible candidates to just over one hundred. Glenn hoped he was included.

One day in January 1959, Lieutenant Colonel John Glenn sat at his neat desk. It was empty of all but the most necessary paper work and one sealed top-secret envelope. Glenn stared at the envelope. He knew in the depths of his rapidly beating heart that this was an invitation to continue on to the next phase of the selection process. But what if it wasn't? Glenn slit the edge open and read his orders. He was one of the one hundred finalists, and was to report to the Pentagon wearing civilian clothes for a space program briefing. Glenn sat back in his chair with a huge smile on his face. He had made it!

Less than a month later, on February 2, 1959, Glenn and the other astronaut candidates reported to NASA headquarters in Washington, D.C. There they were asked to volunteer for the upcoming space flights NASA was planning. First, there would be suborbital flights that would go into space but would not circle the earth. Then there would be orbital flights that would go far enough into space to achieve orbit around the globe. The men were told that these were very dangerous missions and that they could die in space. They could even die before they left the earth if something went wrong with the rocket during launching. The space program was experimental. It could be a poor career move, leading nowhere. There was a chance the entire program would fail, making the astronauts look ridiculous. On the other hand, if the program was successful, the men would have the ride of a lifetime. They could gain international fame. In fact, there was already talk of an exclusive contract with *Life* magazine, the famed pictorial publication. Because the selected astronauts would receive their usual military pay, these contracts would mean extra income. The men could become financially secure.

Glenn looked over the other finalists — the competition. He knew the risk wouldn't bother any military men offered this chance. Everyone present had experienced grave danger of one sort or another in the past. This was a once-in-a-lifetime opportunity that none of them could pass up. The talk of financial bonuses was only an extra incentive.

But there was some concern about the amount of flying and control the first space pilots would have. It was common knowledge on military air bases across the country that the first space capsules were remote-controlled by tracking stations posted around the world. If an astronaut found himself in immediate danger, there was nothing he could do to control his own destiny. His life was almost totally in the hands of civilians sitting at these earth stations behind control panels. As one military pilot said, the astronauts were nothing more than "Spam in a can." In other words, there was none of the flight control to which these pilots were accustomed. Ironically, though NASA was looking for topnotch pilots, the men selected would be doing very little piloting!

John Glenn shared this concern but believed that if he were allowed involvement in the program, he could change it. Outer space was too close for him to stop now. To the man who'd grown up on dreams of flying, the dream of a lifetime was within his grasp. It would be the most incredible ride imaginable. He volunteered. Over the next few months, the number of candidates dwindled. Slowly, painstakingly, comparing one candidate with another, NASA officials narrowed the list down to thirty-two possible choices. John Glenn was on that list.

7

The Chosen Seven

THROUGHOUT THE EARLY months of 1959, the thirty-two astronaut candidates were subjected to an incredible array of painful, grueling physical and psychological tests. Shuffled between Langley Air Force Base in Virginia and Wright-Patterson Air Force Base in Ohio, they were poked, prodded, analyzed, and examined by every kind of specialist imaginable. In fact, they were treated no better than test animals in experimental laboratories.

In one test, the candidate's hand was strapped down. A long needle was inserted into the base of his thumb and electric volts were passed through the needle, making the candidate's fist clench and unclench involuntarily. Other tests were designed to see how the men responded when they were deprived of light and sound for long periods of time.

The psychological tests, meanwhile, had no right or wrong answers. For instance, the candidates were questioned about early childhood. Did they take risks needlessly? Were they afraid of death? Nonetheless, the answers the men gave were carefully charted so as to gain insight into their personality and mental stability.

The astronaut candidates had reservations about the purpose of such testing, but Glenn kept his criticism to himself. He suspected that just being able to tolerate the tests would be looked on positively by NASA officials. He noticed that if a candidate wanted to know the purpose of a test, he was greeted with cold stares instead of answers. If a candidate was annoyed by the poking and prodding, or complained loudly, that was charted, too. Glenn chose not to ask questions. Rather, he smiled amiably. As he was passed from lab technician to physician back to lab technician, he chatted and grinned, whistled and hummed. He proved he was happy to be in the running.

NASA administrators wanted the candidate selection process kept secret. They didn't want to be slowed by the curious public or by the media. Some of the candidates expressed discomfort with the secrecy, thinking it unnecessary, even silly. Glenn played along without a word. Like the other candidates, he hid from newspaper and television reporters, dressing in plain civilian clothes as he flew across the country from one testing facility to another. As he boarded commercial airplanes, Glenn would dress casually in sport shirts and pants, hoping to look like a military pilot on leave. Once in a while the marine pilot would wear a bow tie and suit, hoping to pass for a traveling salesman.

As other potential astronauts got fed up with the elaborate testing and were disqualified, Glenn accepted the tests almost cheerfully. He drew pictures for the psychologists to analyze, and filled in the dots for standardized learning tests. He happily rolled up his sleeve for blood tests. He stood still for X rays and probes. He answered even the most inane questions graciously, as though pleased the psychologist or physician had thought to ask. He wasn't going to do or say anything that would jeopardize his chances.

On April 1, 1959, at NASA headquarters in Washington, D.C., the names of the chosen seven were announced at a press conference: Malcolm Scott Carpenter, Leroy Gordon Cooper, Jr., Virgil "Gus" Grissom, Walter M. Schirra, Jr., Alan B. Shepard, Jr., Donald K. "Deke" Slayton, and, yes, John Herschel Glenn. As the seven filed in in alphabetical order to sit at a long table at the front of the room, bright lights suddenly snapped on, casting a sharp glare into the astronauts' eyes. Television cameras whirred. Flashbulbs popped as photographers crouched and snapped. Reporters trying to meet their deadlines grabbed the astronauts' brief biographies being passed around by NASA press relations personnel and dashed off for phones to call in their stories. Questions were being hurled at Glenn and his comrades from all corners of the room.

Glenn was surprised that the room was so full of

people. He also noticed his fellow astronauts become increasingly uncomfortable with the attention. Each was asked how his wife and family felt about his planned space adventures. Most responded simply that their families supported them. Slayton said that his family hadn't had much say in the matter. Glenn, on the other hand, made it clear that he'd talked to his family about his decision. "I don't think any of us could really go on with something like this if we didn't have pretty good backing at home, really," he said. "My wife's attitude toward this has been the same as it has been all along through all my flying. If it is what I want to do, she is behind it. The kids are, too, a hundred percent."

The astronauts were also asked, much to their surprise, about their religious beliefs. Again, they mumbled quick responses.

Glenn had a clearheaded answer ready: "I think we are very fortunate that we have, should we say, been blessed with the talents that have been picked for something like this. Every one of us would feel guilty, I think, if we didn't make the fullest use of our talents in volunteering for something like this, that is as important as this to our country and the world in general right now."

Glenn took such questions in stride, even as the other astronauts grew increasingly uncomfortable. They started giving shorter and shorter answers, while Glenn responded more thoughtfully and humorously. As the conference progressed, they all realized that the reporters held them in awe. It occurred to Glenn that he was one of seven men being

John Glenn was one of seven astronauts chosen in 1961 to participate in Project Mercury, and quickly came to be seen as the leader of the group. Front row, left to right: Walter (Wally) Schirra, Donald ("Deke") Slayton, Glenn, and Malcolm (Scott) Carpenter. Back row, left to right: Alan B. Shepard, Virgil (Gus) Grissom, and Leroy G. Cooper.

honored, not for something they had done, but for something they were about to do.

The reporters quickly learned that all the astronauts were married with children. The youngest was Cooper, at twenty-nine. Glenn, at thirty-nine, was the oldest. It's possible that age made the bow-tied, clean-cut Glenn stand out as the leader of the group. More likely, it was Glenn's ability to handle even silly questions with grace and ease. Whatever the reason, the media quickly labeled Glenn the astronauts' leader.

Then the reporters asked, "Could I ask for a show of hands of how many are confident that they will come back from outer space?" The clear implication was that those who went up might not come back alive. For the astronauts, this was an easy question to answer; they were well aware that they were embarking on a life-threatening mission. Glenn quickly raised both hands. Flashbulbs went off and reporters chuckled as they jotted notes. Every astronaut at the table had raised his hand.

The conference ended and the astronauts walked from the room. Now they would get down to the serious business of training. *No one will train harder than me,* thought Glenn. He was determined to be the first American in space. Typically, he set out to prove to NASA officials that he was the man for the job. He wanted to show them he had "the right stuff," as writer Tom Wolfe would later describe it in his book of the same name.

The astronauts were expected to be responsible for maintaining their own physical well-being. A fully equipped gym was at their disposal at Cape Canaveral, Florida, where most of their training would take place. Glenn worked out harder and longer than the other six, and made sure he was *seen* working out. Mornings, while the other astronauts were still asleep or just getting started, the smiling Glenn could be seen jogging around the training facility's parking lot.

He attended every class and conference, every meeting. He learned about every piece of equipment and gauge used on the space capsule and in the control room. Glenn and his fellow astronauts inspected and tested the *Mercury* capsules. They were involved in redesign as they demanded the ability to override automatic pilot systems and to control the capsule in flight. They designed a large windshield to replace two almost useless portholes in the original capsule design. When the other astronauts took some time off, relaxed, and maybe even got a little rowdy, Glenn was in his room studying.

Training was intensive and exhausting. But if Glenn felt it, he never let on. He spent hours spinning and whirling again in the centrifuge, which was now being used to simulate up to twelve times the force of gravity experienced on earth. Physicists had determined that rocketing through the earth's atmosphere would increase gravity to nine G's, or nine times earth's gravity. As Glenn, sometimes wearing an orange flight suit, other times suited in full space gear, spun faster and faster, he could feel added weight on his chest and pressure on his eyes, as though they were caving in. Glenn and the other pilots called this the "eyeballs out" position. As if it were some amusement-park ride, the centrifuge would slow down, only to spin again in the opposite direction.

Classroom instruction familiarized Glenn with flight operations in space, geology, astronomy, computer use, guidance systems, navigation, flight mechanics, physics, and meteorology. In addition, he learned about every nook and cranny of the space capsule. He specialized in the cockpit layout, and made significant contributions to the plan and mapping of all the controls and equipment.

He also learned about the complex and cumbersome space suits each astronaut would wear in orbit. Before Glenn could even get into the suit, he was attached to sensors that would constantly feed information on his body's reaction back to the control center. Then he climbed into space underwear, which looked more or less like long underwear. The next layer was the air-cooled space suit. Then Glenn was hooked up to a portable oxygen unit. He placed his helmet on his head while a technician attached special chest and wrist mirrors to him. These allowed him greater visibility out of the capsule's tiny porthole. This ritual was performed almost daily until every detail became second nature.

Because no one knew what to expect in space, Glenn and the others were subjected to merciless heat and cold while clothed in these pressure suits. Since the suits also limited the astronauts' ability to move, getting in and out of the capsule had to be practiced over and over for them to become adept at moving through small spaces with all their equipment on. In particular, they had to learn to be careful not to dislodge the air tube running from the suit to a portable oxygen unit.

In order to experience weightlessness, the astronauts were flown in T-135 jets specially outfitted with windows and internal padding. At speeds in excess of 600 miles per hour, the four-engine jets would flip over, creating up to ten minutes of simulated weightlessness. As the jet flipped again and again, Glenn and the others adapted their movements to zero-gravity. Glenn quickly learned that even throwing a ball became a challenge — it would merely float from his hands. The amazed astronaut watched as liquid floated from a container, then hung in the air. Eating food was an entirely new experience, and Glenn and the others were warned that even crumbs could create a serious hazard if they jammed the control panel as they floated around the cabin of the capsule.

NASA foresaw just about every potential disaster. In case the astronauts had to eject from the capsule, they received parachute training over the open ocean. They spent days rolling and tumbling in the ocean in case they had to emerge, underwater, from the space capsule. In case they landed in the desert, the astronauts were given survival training in the deserts of Nevada, where they learned to find water and food and to protect themselves from the scorching sun. Likewise, they were sent to the Panama Canal Zone for a lesson or two at the Tropical Survival School. The astronauts were to be trained for every possible situation, bar none.

As the astronauts continued their training through 1959 and into 1960, NASA continued its space experiments, sending unmanned satellites in orbit. In 1960, a chimpanzee named Ham made his first suborbital flight for the United States. Then, in April 1961, the Soviet Union sent the first man into space. Cosmonaut Major Yuri A. Gagarin made one orbit around the earth, in the process sending a new wave of alarm across America that the United States was still woefully behind in the space race.

As the pace of training increased, many of the astronauts stayed at the officers' quarters at Cape Canaveral on weekends, rather than return home to their families. Glenn, though, missed his time with Annie and the children. He worried about them and felt guilty about his long absences. Did they miss him? Did they need him at home? The time he was able to spend with his family was very important to him. While the other astronauts let off steam in Cape Canaveral's night spots, Glenn drove home to be with his family.

It was getting harder and harder to see them. He was traveling throughout the country on a regular basis, checking out the space products and components that were being manufactured. Glenn and the other astronauts were also called upon to perform public-service functions. As America's newest heroes, they were expected to accept these added duties willingly because they gave the space program positive media coverage. All of this, however, cut drastically into their family life.

At one point Annie came down to the Cape. She stood at the bow of a naval carrier and watched contentedly as Glenn practiced underwater escape drills from a practice capsule. That summer, Glenn was seen carrying out his duties with his son, David, shadowing his every move. David jogged on the beach alongside his father, dressed in a white T-shirt and dark shorts. As Glenn trained on simulators, he'd look over and grin at the awed expression on his fourteen-year-old son's face.

In the course of their training, Glenn often took it upon himself to remind his fellow astronauts of their responsibility to the space program and their country. This was an extremely important commitment they had made, he would tell them. But some of the astronauts felt that Glenn was out of line with such talk. Who was he to tell them what to do? They thought he was taking the role the press had granted him as leader of the astronauts a little too seriously. In fact, some of the astronauts felt Glenn was too preachy, too much of an "altar boy" or a "goody-goody." Glenn knew that he wasn't always popular because of this. But in the popular press, Glenn was the odds-on favorite to be the first American in space.

The final decision was left up to the astronauts, though, in a vote among themselves. The other astronauts certainly considered Glenn a capable and dedicated member of the team. Many considered him a close friend. But John Glenn's push to be the best hadn't won many points with them. On January 19, 1961, the first ride was awarded to Alan Shepard.

Glenn never demonstrated his disappointment publicly. He applauded the program as a team effort. He acknowledged Shepard's role graciously. But at home, Glenn settled into a funk. Dave would try to coax his father out of silent moods and dark moments, but with no success. Annie tried to get her husband to join the family at backyard barbecues around the neighborhood, only to be greeted with sullen looks and silence. Glenn knew, however, that he had to fight these feelings. He was a team player and he was determined to give his all for the team. By the time of the first flight, Glenn's humor had returned enough for him to sneak a sign into Shepard's cramped space capsule. It read "No Handball Playing."

The launch was scheduled for May 5, 1961. As the sun rose that day, a pink glow spread across the launch pad, making the orange-metal scaffold surrounding the massive Redstone rocket appear a deep red. To John Glenn, it was a perfect day for a space flight. Though he still wished he were the astronaut, he worked diligently to make sure everything would go smoothly for his colleague. As Shepard's backup pilot, Glenn had been involved with all the details leading up to this moment.

Just before he closed the capsule's hatch, Glenn leaned down and wished his compatriot a safe journey. Then he closed the heavy, bolted door on his fellow astronaut and made the long return from the

77

top of the scaffold to the control-center blockhouse, where he would be in radio contact with the first American to make a suborbital flight.

As he entered the building, Glenn looked back once more at the majestic white rocket. It stood boldly in streams of light from white spotlights that dimmed against the lightening sky. From here the black titanium space capsule, perched on top of the explosive giant, looked small and fragile.

At that moment, it didn't matter at all to Glenn who was in the capsule. He felt his skin tingle as he viewed the awesome sight. He was proud to be involved in such a historic project, and right now, he had important work to do.

8

You Have Orbit

ALAN SHEPARD'S *MERCURY 4* flight went off without a hitch. From the fiery launch to the dramatic splashdown, everything went as planned for the first American in space. Upon his return to earth, Shepard was treated like a conquering hero, and no one was happier for him than John Glenn.

On July 21, 1961, Gus Grissom became the second American to go up in space. Grissom's *Mercury 5* flight, like Shepard's, was suborbital, and once again the backup man was John Glenn. This flight, too, was successful, although during splashdown the capsule's hatch opened too early, and Grissom had to be fished out of the sea. He was unhurt but disappointed and embarrassed. The capsule sank, preventing NASA from performing a large part of its post-flight analysis.

On August 6, 1961, fate worked to assure Glenn of his place in history. On this date, the United States's greatest rival, the Soviet Union, launched its second cosmonaut into space. Cosmonaut Gherman S. Titov completed a sixteen-orbit flight that sparked an uproar in the United States. From the West Coast to the East, people wondered how NASA could have allowed the Soviets to move so far ahead in the space race. Many feared that the first country to conquer space would conquer the world. Since it looked as if the Soviet Union was quickly conquering space, fear of the Communists grew. NASA received heavy pressure and inspiration from newly elected President John F. Kennedy to recoup the ground the U.S. space program had lost. It wasn't long before John Glenn was named as the next astronaut to go into space.

Little did Glenn know that, although his flight would come third in the series of *Mercury* project flights, he would become one of the most famous astronauts in the world. Unlike the first two pilots, he would be the first United States astronaut to successfully achieve orbit around the earth.

Glenn was ecstatic and impatient when he learned that December 20 through the 29 were reserved as possible dates for the proposed flight. As his training stepped up, he became entrenched in flight-simulation practice and procedure reviews. Glenn's enthusiasm was tempered only briefly when technical delays postponed the flight until after New Year's Day. He knew that sooner or later he'd go up. He told himself that all the delays only meant he would be more thoroughly prepared when the time finally came. He concentrated even harder on preparations.

On a cold January day in 1962, John Glenn sat with his family along the banks of Virginia's Great Falls. The chilly wind chafed against Glenn's face. He noticed the brilliant blue of the sky as soft clouds floated past. Usually a day with his family filled him with great contentment, but he wasn't smiling that day. Rather, the serious-faced father thought only of his wife and two children. He wanted his family to know that there was a chance he could die on this mission, and that this was something he'd known from the start. He knew that somewhere along the line an astronaut would lose his life in the quest for space. Glenn had brought home mock-ups of the space capsule, which resembled a garbage can full of dials and wires, so that he could show the family the craft in which he would be flying. Together, they had charted Glenn's proposed course on a world map. They'd discussed Glenn's mission and the experiments he hoped to complete. But until then, no one had talked about the possibility of death.

Carolyn and David responded with quiet seriousness, their brown eyes stunned, as they listened to their dad explain that he didn't want them to blame anyone in the event that he didn't return. He didn't want them to be bitter. He wanted his children to understand that this flight was a chance he was taking because he believed in his country and his country's space program. It offered new hopes and horizons for all humanity. His children shouldn't blame him, his country — not even God — if the flight should fail.

Glenn reported back to the Cape, ready to continue the grueling training schedule. But his flight continued to be delayed. Announced flight dates were canceled and rescheduled again and again, as weather conditions and technical difficulties continued to plague the mission, now named *Friendship* 7. Each time, Glenn summoned up his courage, only to be told "not today." The number of cancellations rose to five, then eight.

When the delays were caused by the weather, Glenn was usually told before he boarded the capsule. One time, he lay strapped inside the capsule for five hours and fifteen minutes while ground control waited for cloudy skies to clear. With twenty minutes to go before lift-off, the heavy clouds refused to budge and the mission was scrubbed one more time.

On more than one occasion, Glenn lay inside the capsule, waiting for the countdown, only to be told that there were technical problems. He was instructed to return to the ground and wait for another day. At one point, as the delays dragged on, Dr. Constantine Generals, Jr., a NASA medical researcher, said that the strain of all the cancellations was so great that another astronaut should be assigned to this mission. Glenn was relieved when nobody followed up on that recommendation.

The strain was taking its toll back home, too, where Annie and the kids watched on television.

After one delay, Vice-President Lyndon Johnson, who was the White House representative to the space program, sent word that he wished to visit the Glenn family to offer his regrets. He expected to do so in the presence of television cameras. Annie Glenn was tired and tense, and wanted no part of it. In addition, she was a stutterer, and such a stressful situation would only make things worse. She also wasn't about to let anyone use her family for publicity. But Johnson was being quite forceful. Annie called her husband.

A tired and sweaty Glenn had just shed his pressurized suit and was headed toward the showers. Summoned to the phone, he listened as Annie, by now extremely upset, explained in her stuttering speech that Johnson was attempting to force national attention on her and the children. John Glenn wasn't happy. He didn't want to have his family pushed around like that. He shouted into the phone that whatever Annie wanted was fine with him. He'd back her up all the way. Glenn hung up the phone and went off to get cleaned up. When he came back he learned that the vice-president had left.

February 20, 1962 came dark and early for John Glenn. He awoke at about one-thirty in the morning, a half-hour before he was scheduled to get up. The restless marine listened to the silence and reviewed flight procedures in his mind. He wondered if this would be the day his flight would finally be a "go." Thinking back to all the scrubbed missions, it was hard to get excited. NASA flight surgeon Bill

Douglas slipped into the room and leaned against the top bunk of the double-deck bed. He informed the astronaut that the weather was good but not great. Glenn, arms crossed behind his head, lay in the dark bed and asked questions about conditions. The count to launch, said Douglas, was moving right along. Scott Carpenter, Glenn's backup pilot, had checked the capsule. Everything looked good. Glenn rose from the quiet bed to again prepare to soar.

Glenn ate a breakfast of steak, scrambled eggs, jellied toast, Postum, and orange juice. With Douglas's help, he dressed in the silver pressure suit. As he helped Glenn with his wrist mirrors and straps, Douglas slipped the oxygen hose into his office fish tank to check the air supply. Glenn asked Douglas if he had noticed that his fish were floating belly-up in the tank. Douglas gasped and turned to the tank. The fish were fine. Glenn chuckled and continued adjusting his suit straps.

As he walked from the hangar to a waiting van, Glenn was applauded and cheered by the NASA ground crew. Completely suited up and carrying a portable oxygen tank, Glenn walked proudly and acknowledged the show of support from his team. Everyone sensed that that day would be the day.

NASA officials appeared tense as they readied the unwavering Glenn. As he was driven to the launch pad, Glenn peered through the van's window at his mammoth spacecraft. The Atlas rocket, outlined in bright spotlights against the dark sky, stood in regal glory. The gantry tower looked like a giant orange

The Bettmann Archive

Glenn nestled into his Mercury spacecraft in preparation for his 1962 mission. The Soviet Union had already beaten the United States into orbital flight with the successful launching of Cosmonaut Gherman Titov on August 6, 1961. Still, Glenn's historic orbit of the Earth placed the United States in good stead in the space race, as Americans felt renewed confidence in the country's space program.

cage surrounding the rocket. Atop all this sat the tiny space capsule, an American flag painted on its side.

Before long, Glenn had climbed in an elevator to the capsule, seventy feet above Launch Pad Fourteen. He squeezed through the porthole and stationed himself on the form-fitting couch. Hands and arms reached into the capsule and faces appeared before the tiny hatch opening as technicians and crew members wished him luck. *This'll finally be a go,* hoped Glenn, as reports filtered over the radio that the weather was clearing. As the hatch was lifted into place, a bolt broke. Glenn waited patiently as it was fixed. Then, with a growing realization that this really was going to be the day he'd see space, Glenn watched as the hatch was closed and bolted shut. Shortly, loud horns blew the warning that all personnel should clear the gantry. Glenn checked the time. It was almost eight o'clock in the morning.

He looked over his controls. To the left were hand controls that reminded Glenn of the wagon handles he'd played with as a child. These were used to override automatic controls. If he needed to, Glenn could turn the top handle to even out the capsule's up and down motion, called the pitch. Another controlled the yaw, or side-to-side motion of the capsule. Yet another handle controlled the roll. More than fifty toggle switches dotted the control panel. These, too, were used to override automatic pilot controls, to fire the smaller rockets needed for re-entry, to open manually the landing parachute, to control the capsule's atmospheric functions, and to maintain radio contact. Glenn checked each. If he needed to, he could operate these switches in total darkness.

As Alan Shepard began the countdown, Glenn felt a tingle across his scalp. It was eerie to know he was sitting on top of a rocket that, at any moment, would be blasting off, causing over 300,000 pounds of thrust to shoot the *Friendship 7* toward space. Still, Glenn's respiration and heartbeat barely changed. As the countdown reached ten seconds, the gantry pulled away from the spacecraft and Glenn could see patches of blue sky among clouds through his window.

"May the good Lord ride all the way!" radioed Scott Carpenter from the blockhouse, where he was operating as backup pilot. From Mercury Control Center, the count continued: "Three, two, one, zero!"

Glenn felt the engines fire up. The entire rocket shook solidly beneath him. A gentle surge let him know he was on his way. The time was nine-forty-seven A.M. Glenn looked at his control panel and announced to control center, "Roger. The clock is operating. We're under way!"

In the rearview mirror at the bottom of his window, Glenn could see the blue horizon turning as the rocket rolled to the right. He felt a steady increase in G-forces, and the growing vibrations shook him as his ears filled with a dull roar from the engines. "Little bumpy about here," he reported.

The vibrations increased in intensity, causing the

entire rocket to shudder violently as the aircraft encountered its maximum point of resistance. Glenn could see a white vapor trail streak out his window. The rocket was plowing through the earth's atmosphere. The shuddering slowed.

"We're smoothing out some now," he said, relieved that the spacecraft had survived maximum stress. He announced that the cabin pressure was holding steady. Then Glenn felt pressure increase on his chest, pressing him back into his seat. At its strongest point, Glenn knew he would weigh almost half a ton. But this was a sensation he'd experienced many times on the practice centrifuge. He knew it wasn't going to be too bad.

Acceleration dropped rapidly as two of the three main Atlas engines cut off. The spacecraft shook for a moment, and then Glenn saw the spent engines float away from the spacecraft. An escape tower attached to the craft drifted away next. Outside earth's atmosphere, he wouldn't need it. Just as the automatic pilot released the tower, Glenn touched the switch that would have manually ejected it.

"I am *go*!" said Glenn. "Capsule is in good shape. . . . All systems are *go*!" he added.

As the capsule pitched down briefly, Glenn got his first view of the earth, in vivid blues and greens. He saw fat, white clouds stretched across the Atlantic Ocean. The spacecraft pitched up again. Above him, space was velvety black.

Then, suddenly, Glenn felt as if he were being pitched forward, head over heels, as the clamp ring holding the spacecraft and the remaining Atlas rocket together was released by the firing of two small rockets. *Wow!* Glenn thought. *Those rockets really boot you off!*

For the first time, Glenn felt as though he were being lifted off his seat. What this meant was simple: He had reached zero gravity.

"Zero G, and I feel fine," he reported to mission control, as the capsule tilted sideways 180 degrees. Glenn was facing backward, the normal position for space flight. He saw the Atlas rocket hanging in midair, slowly moving lower and farther away. Next Glenn heard the best words he'd ever heard. "Seven, you have a *go!*" The spacecraft was performing well and was ready to begin its orbit.

As the craft cruised around the world at 17,545 miles per hour, ranging in altitude from 98 miles to 162 miles above the earth, Glenn maintained radio contact with stations situated in several different countries. Glenn would also lose contact with earth for periods of time. Now the voice of Al Shepard faded out. It was replaced with the voice of Gus Grissom, stationed in Bermuda. Glenn continued to report on equipment and the craft. Turning the handles to his left, Glenn controlled the pitch and yaw of the capsule.

He flew over the Canary Islands, then reached under his periscope to retrieve flight-plan cards and a map. As he approached each new station, he reported on the bank of fuses above his arm. Then he reported on the position of each toggle switch to the left of the center panel. Finally, he reported on supplies and fuel levels. As he completed this particular check, he glanced through the periscope.

"The horizon is a brilliant blue," he said. "There, I have the mainland in sight at the present time . . . and have the Canaries in sight out through the window."

As Glenn traveled backward, he observed everything in his periscope first, before he viewed it in his window. As he passed over Africa, he took pictures of a dust storm swirling across a brown desert.

Physicians at the tracking station in the Canary Islands requested that Glenn go through some tests to determine motion sickness during weightlessness. With his heavy helmet in place, Glenn shook his head back and forth and up and down. He reported he experienced no nausea. Glenn took his own blood pressure, which physicians reported was about normal. Then Glenn checked his eyesight with a little chart stuck on the instrument panel. All was fine.

As he passed over the Indian Ocean, Glenn turned to his left to watch the first of three orbital sunsets. Looking through a filter, he stared at the round, yellow fireball as it sank over the dark horizon. Before the sun touched the horizon, it lit both sides of the curving landscape brightly. The red light was intense against the darkness of space and the dim earth below. The sun looked as though it had melted, turning the area pink and orange. Colors spread across the horizon before disappearing below the rim of the earth. With the sun gone, a yellow and pale blue band surrounded the earth, which appeared as a black hole. Then there was nothing. The stars shone above in perfect brilliance.

The people of Perth, Australia, and nearby towns turned on their lights to salute the American astronaut as he passed over them during the night. From orbit, these lights appeared to Glenn as twinkling spots far below. "The lights show up very well, and thank everybody for turning them on, will you?" Glenn asked.

Glenn flew across the Pacific Ocean. Opening the visor of his helmet, he squeezed a tube of applesauce into his mouth. He reported no problem eating. NASA officials had been concerned that weightlessness would be a problem even with food sucked from special tubes. Glenn reported he'd noticed that his arms moved slowly and effortlessly in zero gravity. When he'd wanted to free his hands while taking pictures, he merely set the camera in the air and retrieved it from the same spot moments later.

Glenn described the magnificent sunrise over Asia. Looking from the periscope to his window, he was surprised to see what at first appeared to be a field of stars so thick he couldn't find the horizon. He realized these luminous specks weren't stars. It was as though he were walking backward through a field of fireflies!

The luminous yellow-green particles danced before Glenn's eyes as he stared out the spacecraft window. As the craft cruised through space, the particles drifted slowly backward. There appeared to be millions of them. Occasionally they swirled up around the capsule and across the window. Glenn noted that they looked white, like a piece of fluff or a snowflake. He wondered if they were caused by the hydrogen peroxide jet streams he had been using to control the capsule's pitch and yaw. He reported the phenomenon to ground control.

Ground control in Canton, Ohio, asked if the particles had made any impact on the capsule. No, Glenn assured them. He tried the hydrogen peroxide jets but didn't see any new particles form.

As the sun rose and the earth background became brighter, the particles became difficult to see. Then they disappeared. Glenn scanned space from his window, trying to see more, but they were gone. Ground control was already calling this the Glenn Effect, as they wondered if the particles were caused by the capsule's cooling system or if they were simply dust particles in sun beams. The existence of these particles remains a mystery to this day.

John Glenn was kept busy as he rounded into his second orbit of earth. He snapped photos and made continuous reports to control centers. As he flew over Mexico, the capsule began to drift, turning to the right. *The autopilot should be taking care of this*, Glenn thought as he manually corrected the yaw. He could hear the pulse of steam as the attitude-control thruster, which jettisoned hydrogen peroxide, came into action. Glenn soon had to repeat this manual control. He reported to the ground that he was reverting to "fly by wire," or manual operation, to control the spacecraft's yaw.

As the sun rose over the earth, light streamed into the capsule. "The sun coming through the window is very warm where it hits the suit," he reported.

Even though Glenn was controlling the craft, it continued to roll. To correct this, he made a 180-degree roll. As he did so, the ground appeared to come up at him. *Just like sitting up front in a Greyhound bus. Boy, that's beautiful,* he thought.

Over Zanzibar, an island off the coast of east Africa, Glenn watched a thunderstorm. Lightening flashed from thick gray and black clouds, lighting the sky. He reported that the cloud tops glowed like light bulbs wrapped in cotton.

As Glenn passed over the Indian Ocean, he received a message from Mercury Control Center to keep his landing-bag switch in the Off position. Glenn checked the switch. It was off. A few minutes later, the same message was repeated. Glenn responded, "Affirmative. Landing-bag switch is in the center Off position."

"You haven't heard any banging noises or anything of this type?" asked the voice of ground control.

"Negative."

As Glenn flew to the next checkpoint, he was again asked about his landing bag. Again, he responded that all was fine. Glenn wondered why ground control was so concerned about the landing-bag switch. He reassured himself that the scientists on earth were probably trying to ascertain if the particles could have come from the landing bag. He continued his peaceful journey around the world.

He passed over the United States in eight minutes and reported that everything was fine. He himself felt good, too. In fact, Glenn was thoroughly enjoying the free feeling of space. Despite the high speeds, Glenn felt as though he were merely floating. There was no friction between tires and road, as a driver would experience driving down a county highway. There was no tail wind, as there would be flying a plane or jet in earth's atmosphere. The only sense of speed Glenn saw was from watching the giant orb move away below. Countries were speeding away almost as fast as they appeared.

Glenn enjoyed his second sunset. He noticed that the capsule's window was full of dirt that looked like smoke residue. Some of the specks looked like smashed bugs.

Once more, Glenn was asked about the position of his landing-bag switch. Maybe, he thought, this had something to do with the fact that he had to operate manually the capsule's pitch and yaw. Again, he chose not to worry.

Over Johannesburg, South Africa, Glenn saw heat lightning striking out from amber clouds. As he passed over the Indian Ocean, Glenn checked the time. He had been in space for almost three hours and fifty-nine minutes. "I want you to send a message to the commandant of the U. S. Marine Corps, Washington. Tell him I have my four hours' required flight time in for the month and request a flight chit be established for me."

A voice from the ground laughed at Glenn's request that he receive the extra pay allotted military pilots for the minimum monthly flying time. "Roger. Will do. Think they'll pay it?"

Glenn settled back to watch the sunrise. As before, the black space before the window filled with tiny yellowish-green particles. The sun reached its full brilliance and the particles disappeared. Glenn began to prepare for re-entry to the Earth's atmosphere.

As Glenn stowed away his equipment, he continued to control manually the spacecraft's attitude. Over Hawaii, the astronaut finally learned the reason for all the concern over his landing-bag switch.

"We have been reading an indication on the ground of deployment of your landing bag. Cape would like you to check this by putting the landing-bag switch in an auto position and see if you get a light. Do you concur with this?"

A cold sensation ran up John Glenn's back. He knew what would happen to him if the spacecraft's landing bag was deployed, or made ready for use, at that point. The landing bag was under the heat shield on the outside of the wide, rounded bottom of the space capsule. Made of glass fibers, the heat shield was there to absorb the overwhelming 1,000-degree heat of re-entry. After the capsule had safely completed re-entry, and not before, the heat shield was supposed to fall away. Only then should the landing bag fill to right the capsule in the ocean if it landed upside down. If the landing bag was deployed, that meant the heat shield had already dropped away, before Glenn needed it. Without it, John Glenn would burn to death as he re-entered the earth's atmosphere.

9

Reentry

GLENN FULLY UNDERSTOOD the seriousness of the problem he faced. He prayed that the control-center computers were giving a false reading. He also hoped that switching the toggle to the automatic position wouldn't worsen the situation. As the Hawaiian Islands passed beneath him, the hesitant astronaut flipped the switch. As quickly as he'd flipped it on, he flipped it off again.

"In automatic position did not get a light, and I'm back in the Off position now," he reported to ground control.

"Roger, that's fine. In that case, re-entry sequence should be normal." The reassuring voice of the Hawaiian control tower faded. No one told Glenn that it wasn't just one control center computer that indicated his landing bag was deployed. Rather, *several* Mercury communication stations around the world were all getting the same red warning light. Each technician observed the flashing button and said a silent prayer that John Glenn would make it safely home.

As Glenn's capsule passed over California, he and the ground-control crew reviewed re-entry procedures. Because no one was sure of the heat shield's status, members of the space team were worried that the capsule would burn up when it passed into the earth's atmosphere. Only John Glenn, unaware of their concern, thought re-entry would be routine. Ground control informed him that there were only thirty seconds until a small pack of retrorockets, or retropack, would automatically fire to slow the *Friendship 7* enough to enter the earth's atmosphere.

Glenn heard a buzzing, and then a yellow light on his right flashed on. This was the warning light notifying him that the retro-sequence was about to begin. "Retro-warning is on," he told Wally Schirra, the astronaut assigned to the California communication station, which was in contact with Glenn as he passed over most of the United States.

Schirra responded. "Leave your retropack on through your pass over Texas." Schirra had been told not to give Glenn any more information than this. Engineers at the Mercury Control Center at Cape Canaveral reasoned that if the heat shield was loose, the retropack, partially positioned over the heat shield, might keep it in place. Still, no one told Glenn of their concern.

Glenn tensed as he watched a green light flash

the retro-sequence. A second green light told him he was in the proper attitude, or position, for re-entry. If Glenn's capsule came into the atmosphere at the wrong pitch or angle, it would cave in on itself from the pressure.

Schirra's voice measured a steady cadence in Glenn's ears. "Five, four, three, two, one, fire!"

Suddenly there was a roar behind Glenn, and he felt as if he and the capsule were being pushed backward. He focused on the instrument panel and fought the violent pitching and rolling. After five seconds he felt another kick, as the second retro-rocket ignited. He fought another wave of rolling and pitching. Five seconds later he felt a third, and final, kick. Glenn looked over the gauges. He was delighted to see that he was holding the capsule on course. The needles on the gauges before him set-tled down as, within twenty-two seconds, the three retrorockets burned out. Looking out the window, Glenn could see that he was on a steady ride into the east. Even though the retrorockets had slowed him a bit, Glenn was hurtling toward the edge of the atmosphere at more than 17,000 miles per hour.

He heard static over the headset, then Schirra's voice. "Keep your retropack on until you pass Texas," he reminded Glenn.

"That's affirmative." A red light on the instru-ment panel reassured Glenn that his retropack had not jettisoned, as it would during a normal re-entry. "Jettison retro is red," he reported. "I'm holding on to it."

As Glenn passed over the West Coast, he continued to steer the speeding capsule. He could see all the way from El Centro, a town in southern California, to the Salton Sea, a river near Seattle, Washington. Irrigated areas of California's Imperial Valley stood out against patches of brown desert.

Glenn heard more static in his headset, then the voice of Al Shepard at Texas ground control. "We are recommending that you leave the retropackage on through the entire re-entry."

John Glenn's worry that something was wrong with the heat shield was reawakened by this significant change in procedure. He wanted to know exactly what was wrong. If his life was about to end in an inferno, he had every right to know. The anxious astronaut was also a bit angry, but he had no choice but to trust Mercury Control Center.

"What's the reason for the change in plans?" he asked. He was greeted with silence.

In the meantime, he had work to do. The retropack was in the way of the periscope, which needed to be retracted for re-entry. Glenn turned the manual crank. He was still waiting for an answer.

"While you're doing that," Shepard said over Glenn's headset, "we are not sure whether your landing bag has deployed. We feel that it is possible to re-enter with the retropackage on. We see no difficulty at this time with that type of re-entry."

The periscope door closed and the worried astronaut was surrounded by the dark. Glenn looked down at the dials and switches before him. He was in the correct position for re-entry. He closed his

A motorcade in honor of Astronaut Colonel John H. Glenn moves up Broadway on March 1, 1962, as New Yorkers pay tribute to a new American hero. Glenn's safe homecoming, and the progress his mission symbolized, reassured millions of Americans that the United States had a firm grip on the space race.

eyes and said a silent prayer. Everything would be
fine if the capsule could only survive the incredible
heat. The astronaut continued to hurtle toward
earth. He would know soon enough.

"*Seven,* this is Cape. We recommend that
you . . . " The voice faded out. Glenn had reached a
stage in the re-entry process during which the
earth's magnetic field made communication impossible. For the next four minutes he would be
completely alone. Manually, Glenn started the capsule revolving slowly in order to ensure that he'd
land accurately. He heard a loud blast as one of the
retropack's stainless-steel straps broke loose. He
could see it dangling in front of the window.

"This is *Friendship Seven.* I think the pack just
let go," Glenn said. But no one heard him.

This is it, Glenn thought as he hit the earth's
atmosphere. He had to fight with the controls in
order to stay on course. All the time he waited to
feel intense heat on his back. If the heat shield was
out of position, this would be the first place Glenn
would feel the inferno.

The long minutes crawled slowly past. A brilliant
orange glow licked at the window. The astronaut
stared as large flaming pieces of metal rushed past.
I'm burning up, he thought. *The capsule is on fire!*
He concentrated on remaining calm. *Watch the
controls,* he thought. *Stay on course.* But it was
difficult, if not impossible, to not concentrate on his
back. Did it feel hot? Was he about to burn? The
friction of the atmosphere forced the capsule to
slow down rapidly. Increasing gravity held him se-

curely. The brilliant orange flame was all around him.

"This is *Friendship Seven*. A real fireball outside." He didn't think anyone could hear him yet. Almost four minutes had passed since he'd been in contact with earth.

Then, a distorted voice from the Cape Canaveral radio tower made his heart leap with gratitude. "How are you doing?"

The fire outside faded slowly. "Oh," he answered, "pretty good." He was still working to control the capsule.

"*Seven*, this is Cape. What's your general condition? Are you feeling pretty well?" asked a concerned Shepard.

"My condition is good, but that was a real fireball, boy! I had great chunks of that retropack breaking off all the way through," Glenn said with obvious relief in his voice.

Outside Glenn's window, the blue canopy of sky had reappeared. At 55,000 feet, he could see the white vapor trails from his descent. At about the same time, he felt the first parachute open. He also noticed that he was feeling uncomfortably warm.

Glenn watched out his window for the larger main chute. His first sight of it was a red-and-white line streaming above. The red-and-white silk filled with air and jerked the capsule up, and Glenn swung back and forth at the end of the line. Looking over his instrument panel, Glenn saw the landing-bag switch. He flipped it on. With a bump, the landing bag deployed, proving that it had never been loose at all, and that the heat shield had been in place all along. Slowly but swiftly, he drifted toward the wide ocean waters. With a gentle splash, the capsule hit the water, then began to bounce and bob.

As the destroyer U.S.S. *Noa* headed for Glenn's capsule, he announced his landing. "This is *Friendship Seven*. I'm very warm. I'm just remaining motionless here trying to keep as cool as possible. I'm extremely warm," he added, with good reason. At its hottest, the interior of the cabin registered 108 degrees.

The *Noa* came alongside. Glenn soon felt a gentle brushing, and then the capsule was hoisted to the destroyer's deck. Glenn sat quietly, the capsule rocking gently with the ship. He was hot, and sweat was pouring out of him. He didn't think he could wait for anyone to help him out. Glenn decided the best thing to do would be to blow the hatch.

He radioed the ship and asked them to clear the area so no one would be hurt. He turned his head away from the door and, with the back of his hand, hit the firing pin. He heard a loud explosion and felt a momentary sting as the firing-pin handle cut into his knuckles. Then he felt hands under his arms, reaching into the capsule to help him out.

As the confident and grinning astronaut stood on the deck, he breathed deeply of the fresh ocean breeze. He felt the air drying his sweat-soaked cheeks. He could taste the salt as he looked out at the friendly sky and gentle ocean. The crew stood on an upper deck, a painted sign welcoming the beaming astronaut home. They announced he was the ship's "Sailor of the Month." A seaman knelt before Glenn, a paintbrush in hand, and traced the astronaut's first footsteps on the *Noa*'s deck. The first thing Glenn did was call his wife, Annie, in Maryland, and let her know he was home, safe. It would be a few days until the astronaut would see his family. NASA officials planned to ship Glenn to the Bahamas, where he'd rest a few days before returning to the United States mainland.

Glenn was transported to the U.S.S. *Randolph*, where he was to undergo a debriefing and a thorough physical exam. That evening, Glenn found a quiet seat on deck. Relaxing, his feet up on the ship's rail, the joyous Glenn watched his fourth sunset of the day as he tape-recorded his recollections.

He was home again. During his four-hour-and-fifty-six-minute flight, John Glenn had experienced what no other American had yet experienced. From space, he had seen the earth in all its gentle beauty. He had circled it three times and survived a fiery re-entry. The nation rose in celebration to give John Glenn a hero's welcome.

The flight was an impressive triumph for the United States. It reassured millions of Americans that the United States had a firm grip on the space race. Across the country, millions watched on television as the red-haired astronaut's historic flight ended. Many cheered. Some wept with pride as they realized that this was the first step toward traveling to the moon. President Kennedy ex-

105

pressed the nation's hope and pride when he said, "This is the new ocean, and I believe the United States must sail on it and be in a position second to none."

The day's cheering turned into weeks and months of celebration. Glenn was welcomed back to Florida by streets lined with crowds shouting congratulations, some with tears of joy in their eyes, many waving American flags. He was a guest of honor at the White House. Millions of New Yorkers turned out in pouring rain for a ticker-tape parade. Rain streaming down his face, the proud astronaut and his wife waved from the back of a convertible as they rode down Fifth Avenue. Glenn's safe and triumphant return was celebrated in his hometown with more parades and speeches. He was asked to tour the United States as a spokesman for the space program. The handsome astronaut with his clean-cut image and happy smile was cheered wherever he went. Notably, he always made a point of thanking all who had been on his team and made his space ride possible. Glenn was a team player.

Speaking before a joint session of Congress, Glenn expressed his views of the space program and spoke out strongly on behalf of the nation's space effort.

"We are just probing the surface of the greatest advancements in man's knowledge of his surroundings that has ever been made, I feel," Glenn said. "Knowledge begets knowledge. The more I see, the more impressed I am — not with how much we know, but with how tremendous the areas are that are as yet unexplored." Tears sparkling at the corners of his eyes, Glenn concluded, "As our knowledge of the universe in which we live increases, may God grant us the wisdom and guidance to use it wisely."

Members of Congress responded with a standing ovation. Stunned, Glenn looked out over the crowd. These were some of the most powerful men in the world and they were honoring him! He was overwhelmed with emotion.

As it turned out, John Glenn didn't stay with the space program for very long after his historic flight. Though he toured the country on behalf of NASA, much of his work at NASA centered around administrative duties. At forty, he knew his future opportunities to go back up in space were limited. At the same time, the patriotic American believed he had much to offer his country. Glenn had befriended both President John Kennedy and his brother, Robert, the nation's attorney general. The two Kennedys suggested to Glenn that he might have a future in politics. Glenn thought long and hard about the possibilities. He had already made a contribution to his country, but he wanted to do so much more. The political arena would help him put forward the ideals and goals he had for his country. This was certainly a challenge, and an important one.

But even as he was pulled toward politics, Glenn loved the space program. It, too, presented wide horizons and opportunities. Finally, he decided it

was time to venture into new areas. Glenn wanted
to taste something new and different. The maturing
astronaut reasoned that he could do more for the
space program from a political seat than he could
behind a desk at NASA. The charismatic astronaut
now looked to politics to serve his country. He
would fight valiantly and long for a seat in the U.S.
Senate. Glenn didn't realize he was about to face his
biggest battle to date.

10

The Astronaut Senator

JOHN GLENN HAD failed to be first only once before — when he had been bypassed for the first space flight. He hadn't liked it, but he didn't think it would happen again. After all, he was a national hero. Not even the assassination of his good friend, President John F. Kennedy, in November 1963, could dampen Glenn's enthusiasm. He recalled how J.F.K. had told him he had the right stuff to make a good senator. He had the public recognition, the integrity, the determination, and the self-discipline. In the fall of 1963, Glenn announced his resignation from the U.S. Marine Corps to run for the U.S. Senate as a Democrat from Ohio.

As it turned out, Glenn was defeated, but it wasn't another man who beat him — it was a bathroom fall that took him out of the race before he'd even had a chance to get into the thick of it.

On February 26, 1964, Glenn prepared to shave in the bathroom of the Columbus, Ohio, apartment he had rented for the duration of the campaign. He set his razor on the edge of the sink, then moved to place his soap back in the mirrored cabinet. But Glenn couldn't get the mirror to move properly on the cabinet track. He removed the mirror, cleaned out the tracks, then tried to replace it. The mirror slipped from Glenn's hands. Instinctively, he ducked to avoid being hit by the falling mirror. Despite his athlete's speed and agility, he slipped on a throw rug and fell, hitting his head on the edge of the porcelain bathtub. Glenn lay dazed on the floor, blood pouring from a cut in his temple.

Glenn's campaign staffers heard the crash and ran to his aid. As they tried to raise the former astronaut to a sitting position, unbearable pain and pressure burned through his head. If Glenn tried to look up, the pain increased. Finally, the staff members carried the semiconscious man to a bed and called an ambulance. The candidate was rushed to an area hospital.

Glenn suffered a mild concussion, as well as a buildup of blood and fluid in the left inner ear, which in turn affected his balance and coordination. The bleeding and swelling were causing incredible pain. The inner-ear problem could be taken care of with a great deal of time and patience, but there was a graver concern. Doctors feared that the impact of the fall had caused a potentially fatal blood clot to form on the brain. Annie Glenn and the children were called and rushed to his side.

Glenn awoke in his hospital bed that night to see Annie, Carolyn, and David looking frightened in his darkened room. Even as doctors continued their vigil, constantly checking his eyes for signs of distress, Glenn reassured his family that he would be all right.

The threat of the blood clot soon disappeared, but Glenn still had to overcome the lingering effects of his fall. During the following days, which turned into weeks, then months, the symptoms from the swelling in Glenn's inner ear greatly disrupted his life. At first, even breathing nauseated Glenn. He experienced constant ringing in his ears. The simplest movement caused dizziness and vomiting. The first two weeks, he also experienced chronic headaches, making it impossible to do anything but lie perfectly still in a darkened room. His overall condition was so bad that, initially, he postponed his retirement from the marines. Finally, he dropped out of the Senate campaign.

The former astronaut recuperated slowly. The second week the headaches and ringing decreased. It was a month before Glenn could sit up for two hours at a time. If he held onto both walls and kept his head at a forty-five-degree angle, the graying, tired-looking man could walk short distances along the hospital corridor. Progress was painfully slow. Glenn became withdrawn, and although Annie remained by his side, not even she could ease his depression. He didn't seem interested in anything anymore. By Easter of 1964, all of Glenn's family were concerned. To honor a "fallen warrior," and in recognition of his past work, President Lyndon Johnson promoted Glenn to the rank of colonel.

By the time he returned home, Glenn could maneuver around the house, but had to balance with his hands, wall to wall. The slow recovery continued to wear on Glenn, a man used to activity and adventure. Even when he had been chained to desk work, Glenn had been physically active. Numerous newspapers, reporting on Glenn's slow recovery, recounted Glenn's activities. Up to that point, summers had been spent shooting rapids and backpacking with Robert Kennedy's family. Winters were reserved for skiing in Colorado. Glenn had played handball and racquetball daily. He had run and worked out. Now it was a challenge simply to walk to the kitchen. He began to refer to himself as a "used astronaut," an "ex-politician," and "a depressed area." Unpaid campaign debts added another layer of trouble to his already difficult life.

John Glenn may have been down, but he wasn't out. He worked hard at his physical therapy, and, as he recuperated, he pulled himself out of his depression. Glenn repaid his campaign debts from his personal funds, and obtained a position as a vice president of the board of directors of Royal Crown Cola. In 1965, he was named a NASA consultant. He served as a celebrity delegate at astronautic conventions, giving speeches. He contributed many ideas to Project Apollo, the project whose goal was to land a man on the moon by the end of the decade.

Glenn had made himself contentedly busy. Although the next years were good to Glenn, they weren't without tragic personal losses. In 1966, John Glenn served as a pallbearer at Gus Grissom's funeral. Glenn's fellow astronaut died, along with Roger Chaffee and Ed White, in a fiery explosion on a Cape Canaveral launch pad. In 1968, John and Annie Glenn stood alongside the Kennedy family to bury their friend, Robert Kennedy, who had been shot just after the California Democratic primary. Glenn also suffered the loss of both his parents.

The world was changing. It was now the era of hippies and flower children, teens who spoke of peace and love. It was a time of short skirts and long hair, bell-bottomed jeans and woven headbands. Popular music promoted change and independence. The Beatles sang of "Revolution," the Rolling Stones of becoming a "Street Fighting Man."

Many of the changes worried John Glenn. Although the civil rights movement led by Martin Luther King, Jr., had made great inroads, many people felt there was still a long way to go. That dissatisfaction erupted into unrest and even riots across the nation. At the same time, U.S. involvement in the Vietnam War was also bitterly dividing the country. Many believed the United States had no business participating in a war being fought halfway around the world. Others believed U.S. involvement was necessary to support freedom and democracy, no matter where it was. College students across the country voiced their displeasure with the government through protests and rallies.

Adults, for the most part, promoted the same kind of patriotism they'd felt during World War II. Families, and the country, were divided, as never before.

John Glenn knew he could help the country through these trying times. On May 5, 1970, the forty-nine-year-old former astronaut again announced his candidacy for the U.S. Senate. "Everyone is losing confidence in everything — our foreign policy, our universities, our electoral system — all because we haven't changed things that need changing, and we haven't told people the truth," he said in his announcement. Glenn ran as a Democrat but refused to tow the party line. He refused to support some traditional Democratic Party ideals if he believed they were tied to "special-interest" groups. Glenn wanted peace and believed in a strong military. But he didn't talk specifics or tell the people how he would go about improving things.

Glenn's campaign was poorly organized, which meant that he failed to show up at those functions that gained the best media coverage. He stood for patriotism and peace, but most of the public rarely heard about his beliefs. While his opponents made headlines at large city fundraisers and political rallies, Glenn was in the rural communities shaking hands and promising to speak for the individual. He refused to cultivate the vote of special-interest groups. He didn't want to owe anyone. He wanted to remain independent. In fact, he remained so independent that he was soundly defeated.

Glenn spent the next four years in business. He

remained with Royal Crown Cola and invested in a chain of Holiday Inns.

In 1974, Glenn announced he would make a third try for office. His opponent was Howard Metzenbaum, a self-made millionaire and popular incumbent. Metzenbaum had a large following in Ohio, and a firm grip on the political seat John Glenn wanted. Glenn faced a hard fight if he wanted to win.

This time, Glenn learned from his past mistakes. He ran an organized campaign and dealt directly with the issues. He campaigned visibly and heavily across Ohio. Although his views often contradicted those of the Democratic Party, Glenn's independence worked in his favor this time.

It didn't hurt that Metzenbaum ran a negative campaign attacking, of all things, Glenn's work record. Radio and television ads constantly harped on the fact that Glenn had "never really held a job." Glenn waited until he knew the timing was right, then strongly criticized Metzenbaum in a public debate covered by the media. He cited his military career and early war records, pointing out that he had won no less than five Distinguished Flying Cross medals and twenty-one Air Medals. He said proudly that he'd risked his life to protect his country in two wars. He expounded on his patriotism. He talked about men of valor and courage, making it clear that he was one of them. Glenn talked about the men who had died for their country. The handsome candidate looked intensely at his adversary and, with emotion in his voice, concluded, "I tell you, Howard Metzenbaum, you should be on your knees every day of your life thanking God that there are some men — some men — who held a job. . . . I've held a job, Howard." The audience came to its feet with resounding applause. At election time, John Glenn carried every county in Ohio.

While in office, Glenn has stood for integrity and justice. He has supported consumer protection issues, national health insurance, and health-education funding on a federal level. He believes that the United States, in order to continue as a world power, needs to remain self-sufficient. In working toward that goal, he has supported new offshore drilling for oil and natural gas distribution. Although he has taken a stand against nuclear arms, he supports a strong defensive military. Glenn has said that his most important Senate contribution to date was as author of the Nuclear Nonproliferation Act of 1978. This act prohibits the United States from selling nuclear fuel to any nation that will not guarantee that the fuel will not be used in nuclear weapons. An additional provision of the agreement calls for countries buying the fuel to follow safety regulations set by the International Atomic Energy Agency.

Glenn's official posts as senator have included being a member of the Interior and Insular Affairs Committee, which studies energy legislation, and the Government Operations Committee, which supervises nuclear power and weaponry. He is also honorary chairman of the Astronaut Council in Washington, D.C.

Like many ambitious politicians and public figures, Glenn found himself hearing the call of an office even higher than that of senator. In April 1983, the sixty-one-year-old senator from Ohio announced his candidacy for the United States Presidency, the highest office in the land. Once again, Glenn had chosen to run in a difficult contest. First, the former astronaut had to win the Democratic nomination in the primary elections. Then, if successful, he would face President Ronald Reagan, who was expected to win his second term in the White House.

Campaigning during the primaries, Glenn told audiences that his main Democratic rivals, former Vice-President Walter Mondale and Senator Gary Hart, had not been "tested under fire" as he had been as a marine and an astronaut. This didn't sway enough voters, however, and the senator lost the first few primaries.

Glenn then shifted the emphasis of his speeches toward his goals for the country and the values he shared with the voters. According to some political analysts, though, Glenn spoke in vague terms, never really pinpointing what his goals were. The losing streak continued.

Another blow came when Glenn's campaign began to run out of the funds necessary to run a strong, nationwide effort. Before the Texas, Washington, and Michigan primaries, when other candidates were airing television commercials, the senator was forced to close his campaign offices in those states in an attempt to save money.

Things looked bad for the campaign, but Glenn wasn't going to quit without a fight. His speeches took on new life as he called the country's people to action the same way that candidate John F. Kennedy had more than twenty years before. "No risk is too great for this nation of ours. No price is too big to pay for that kind of future," Glenn said from his podium. "No burden is too strong to bear for the future that we have at stake."

But in fact it was too late. Although Glenn's speeches drew popular support, they weren't enough to carry the states that he needed. Reluctantly, John Glenn was forced to withdraw from the presidential race. Still, he returned to the Senate all the more dedicated to the job at hand.

It may seem surprising that an active, former astronaut would want to spend time in a government office. After all, being a U.S. senator is a desk job. But Glenn doesn't mind. In part, this may be because opportunities to take the stick of superfast military aircraft are still available. In August 1984, for example, he flew a prototype B-1 bomber during a ten-day, fifteen-stop tour of military installations in the western United States. While flying the black, bat-winged, B-1 from Edwards Air Force Base in California's Mojave Desert, the former test pilot performed two aerial refuelings, two landings, and a high-speed, low-altitude run. "It's a very impressive airplane," he commented during the two-and-one-half-hour flight. But the senator from Ohio was forced to give up the stick because he ran out of time — his tight, demanding schedule called for him to move on to his next appearance. Had there been more time, he said, he would have performed a maneuver that would have tested the outer limits of the bomber's capabilities. As the smiling Glenn said, it was a maneuver that would "push the edge of the envelope." One month later, Senator Glenn learned that the same bomber he had flown had crashed when its pilot began the high-risk maneuver that Glenn had wanted to perform.

After winning reelection in 1988 to his fourth term as a U.S. senator, Glenn was chosen to serve as chairman of the United States Senate Committee on Governmental Affairs. As before, he has spent his time dedicated to a variety of causes. One particular concern of his has been to strive for programs that benefit America's youth, whom he sees as being the key to the country's future. Glenn knows that, historically, the United States has survived because of ideals and dreams carried out by the younger generations. For himself, it was a youthful dream to fly. Glenn understands that today's teens may walk on Mars or even live on other planets. But they have to try if they want to succeed. In 1984, he introduced a legislative package called "Volunteers for America," a three-phase educational and career opportunities package for teens and young adults. Although this package never became reality, the idea of a youth volunteer program has been recognized as worthy, and many versions of such programs have been introduced in the Senate since Glenn's proposal.

Glenn was once given the opportunity to comment on his own role in his country's history. His response looked to both the past and the future: "Columbus had an insatiable curiosity, a relentlessly irresistible dream of pushing on beyond the dragons drawn on the margins of his maps. . . . I hope that young people growing up at the end of the twentieth century will follow Christopher Columbus's example and cultivate his curiosity and questioning and develop skills in research and reporting and critical thinking and debating. . . . I hope that every young person will start right now trying always to be friendly and fair with others, and practicing the democracy that is so important to ensure peace, freedom, and security for all the people of the earth."

John Glenn is a man who recognized and fulfilled his boyhood dreams. In his less glamorous, but equally important, role in government, he has worked to create opportunities for others to fulfill theirs.

Other books you might enjoy reading

1. Cipriano, Anthony J. *America's Journey into Space*. Julian Messner, 1979.

2. Furness, Tim. *Man in Space*. Batsford Academic and Educational Limited, 1981.

3. Hill, Robert W. *What Colonel Glenn Did All Day*. The John Day Company, 1962.

4. Van Riper, Frank. *Glenn, the Astronaut Who Would Be President*. Empire Books, 1983.

5. Vogt, Gregory. *A Twenty-fifth Anniversary Album of NASA*. Franklin Watts, 1985.

6. Wolfe, Tom. *The Right Stuff*. Farrar, Straus, Giroux, 1979.

ABOUT THE AUTHOR

Ann Angel is a journalism instructor at Mount Mary College in Milwaukee, Wisconsin. She has written numerous articles for regional newspapers and magazines, has been a contributing editor for *Wisconsin Woman* magazine, and is the author of a novel for young adults, *Real For Sure Sister*. Angel is currently working on a book about the lives and cultures of children in Mexico. She lives in Wauwatosa, Wisconsin, with her husband and four children.